IDEAS FROM FRANCE

This collection charts the rise of French ideas as they have influenced British culture. It offers a guide to the history of structuralist and post-structuralist concepts in philosophy, literature, Marxism, feminism, history and psycho-analysis. The contributors explain with great clarity what has happened to the text, the author and the subject, concentrating in particular on the ideas of Barthes, Foucault, Althusser and Poulantzas. The book grew out of a discussion series and conference held at London's Institute of Contemporary Arts on the occasion of the death of Michel Foucault. The contributors – many of the most eminent expositors and critics of French ideas writing in English – assess the current state of cultural theory in France and its influence in Britain. The contributors are Christian Descamps, Malcolm Bradbury, Jacques Roubaud, Terry Eagleton, Cora Kaplan, Alan Sheridan, Jeffrey Weeks, John Forrester, Peter Dews, Gareth Stedman Jones, Ted Benton, Michèle Barrett, Bob Jessop, Emmanuel Le Roy Ladurie and Peter Burke.

Lisa Appignanesi is Deputy Director of the Institute of Contemporary Arts and head of its programmes in publishing and television.

IDEAS FROM FRANCE

THE LEGACY OF FRENCH THEORY

ICA DOCUMENTS

Edited by
Lisa Appignanesi

'an association in which the free development of each
is the condition of the free development of all'

Free Association Books / London / 1989

Published in Great Britain 1989 by
Free Association Books
26 Freegrove Road
London N7 9RQ

First published by Institute of Contemporary Arts

British Library Cataloguing in Publication Data

Ideas from France: the legacy of French theory:
ICA documents.
1. French thought
I. Appignanesi, Lisa
194

ISBN 1-85343-113-3

Printed and bound in Great Britain by Billing & Sons Ltd, Worcester

CONTENTS

EDITOR'S NOTE

The articles in *Ideas from France* grow out of a discussion series and a conference held at the ICA in November and December 1984. *French Legacies*, the discussion series, was occasioned by the death of Michel Foucault and our desire to pay homage to his work. In thinking through the series, we felt it was perhaps also time to assess that stream of ideas which had made its way from France to Britain and which could loosely be labelled, structuralist and post-structuralist. Psychoanalysis, sexuality, fiction, politics, the structures of knowledge and power – all had been the subjects of a massive theoretical inquiry in France and this inquiry had marked the course of British thinking over recent years. But how did we view this intellectual current now?

The series led us to ask a further question. How did the French themselves now understand the theoretical inquiry of recent years? In pursuit of an answer, the first step seemed to be to hold a conference which brought together French and British writers and thinkers. *Crossing the Channel* did just that and if the discussion which ultimately ensued was only partial, enraged some and confirmed for others their suspicion of what Jacques Roubaud calls the 'theory monster', it was at least a step. The coming years will bring to the ICA more and varied perspectives from France as part of an exchange agreement with the Collège International de Philosophie in Paris.

The articles collected here are only in part a record of the live events. Some contributions lend themselves more readily to the page; all have been edited or substantially revised by their authors. I am grateful to them all for having taken on this extra work. I owe special thanks to Cora Kaplan whose article acts in some way as a response to conference proceedings and provides a view not expressed elsewhere in this text; and to John Forrester who agreed to translate Christian Descamps' and Emmanuel Le Roy Ladurie's texts at break-neck speed.

Lisa Appignanesi

THE PLEASURES AND PITFALLS OF THEORY

PHILOSOPHY IN FRANCE
Christian Descamps

Alive and various, French philosophy, dealing as it does with desire, with class, with writing, with the world, is looked upon by the greater part of English philosophers as an extravagance. Despite repeated efforts, bridges have never remained open for long between our two countries. If history or anthropology ferry easily across the Channel, philosophy — with very few exceptions — seems to get sick on the way. Certainly, there is nothing much in common to be found under this heading in Oxford, Cambridge and Paris. Indeed, there is also a large institutional difference between the countries. In France, Philosophy is taught in secondary schools. From the age of 16 or 17, school students are confronted with the great texts of the classics. Some experiments have even dared to get 12 and 13-year olds to read Plato — and with good results. With utter amazement they then discover the paradoxes of the cave... To be sure, not everything in this grand brew of ideas has always attained the rigour demanded by those in England who wish to build their houses one brick at a time. But when it comes down to it, can the interplay of ideas of ideas ever avoid the instinctual?

Be that as it may, nothing is written on marble and if, ten years ago, French philosophers talked at length about their Holy Trinity, (Marx, Nietzsche, Freud), they have now realised that no synthesis is possible. The latest thing is to play these — already classical — authors against each other. They are still read, they are still worked at, but as if they were Aristotle or the Hume who was capable of awakening one from dogmatic slumbers. This point aside, it is difficult to keep French philosophers together in one single category. What indeed is there in common between the desiring rhizomes of Deleuze and Guattari, the *differance* of Derrida, the postmodern reflections of Lyotard, the archaeology of Foucault, the *simulacra* of Baudrillard, the imaginary of Castoriadis or the poetic epistemology of Serres? No doubt nothing — except perhaps that they all practice with an informed disrespect and have only a limited veneration for the belief in grammar. French philosophical modernity knows how to rediscover metaphysics in physics, poetry in mathematics, desire in history, aporias in the facts of economics. French philosophers often prefer questions of order and disorder, of the simple and the complex, of the prescriptive, of the *simulacrum*, and on top of that, the old questions about the basis of the organisation of human beings in the city, to the epics of science and the therapeutic promises of word-cures.

In fact, what is at issue for the French is living with and after the debris — fertile as it is — of the grand systems which aspired to the unity of science and stride towards better tomorrows, or to the mastery of the future thanks to the laws of the philosophy of history. In fact, the scientificity of science is much in question today, since Science — singular rather than plural, and with a capital letter — can only be a myth of positivism. But what is also at issue is a refusal of a flabby relativism capable only of articulating the fundamental right to differ.

Abundantly curious about science, about art, about philosophy, our epoch sees thousands of little narratives unfolding. None of them harmonise with one another. We now know that the fact of resisting falsification is characteristic of only very restricted domains. What is more, the fact that something is not falsifiable in no way entails definite certainty. At last, we are listening to Bertrand Russell, who wrote: 'Empirical testing can only confirm or infirm propositions which are constructed in the form of *all* or *none*.' In truth, we live in a world where there are swans of every colour!

It is exciting that, within French philosophy, theories struggle against each other. It is also exciting that the professionals once again engage in interrogations of Parmenides or of Heraclitus. Bound as they are to the instinctual, to the historical, to the political, notions of truth have to be constructed afresh each time. It is no longer only a question of opposing the true and the false, but also the noble and the vile. It is not just a question of refuting error, but just as much of opposing stupidity, baseness, imbecilic discourses entirely constructed out of vast, mediocre truths.

French philosophers know that they will never be done with the questions, 'what is to be done, to be known, to be hoped?' Today they give their answers with the force of fictions of our times. In doing so, the philosophers borrow as much from great novelists and painters as from physicists and mathematicians. And that is perhaps why some philosophical works have the force of conviction of certain works of art.

THE IMPACT OF LITERARY THEORY
Malcolm Bradbury

When I was invited to speak to this splendid and culturally significant occasion, this moment of all too rare alliance, I was, I confess, unsure why I was asked. Was it as a critic, or as a writer? Should I speak as a literary theoretician, which I admit in all modesty I sometimes am, or as what used to be called, before Structuralism, a person, a typically non-theoretical civilian Briton to whom acts of theory are only occasional. It is well known that, unlike the French, whose very language is an epistemological discourse, the British in general are strangers to philosophical thought, except perhaps at football matches. Was it possible, in any case, to speak of Structuralist matters at a British public occasion? To most of the British, Structuralism is at most a Cambridge scandal. And yet one has only to dine, as I did last night, on *cuisine minceur,* that minimalist mode of cooking where the plate is so empty one can only contemplate it as an abstraction, to see that it has, however obliquely, an impact on British life. No, it was discussable, but how was I being asked to discuss it?

However, when I saw in the programme that I was listed as the renowned author of such works as *Skipping Westward,* presumably one of my more carefree and lighthearted books, and *The History of Man,** presumably one of my more complete and compendious, that I realized that in some fashion I was expected to talk about the gap between the signifier and the signified. I then recalled that I was the first person to introduce to the British reading public — a notion itself so vague that, reflecting on it, Wolfgang Iser invented the notion of the imaginary reader — the works of Henri

---

*Malcolm Bradbury is alluding here to a misprint in ICA publicity materials which, in flattering fashion, advertised him as the author of *The History of Man,* rather than *The History Man. Skipping Westward* is, of course, *Stepping Westward.*

Mensonge. Mensonge, you will recall, is the French scholar, philosopher and bon vivant now rightly recognized in all advanced quarters as the Structuralist's Structuralist, or the Deconstructionist's Deconstructioner. Alas, though 16 years have now passed since his key work *La fornication comme acte culturelle* appeared in Paris (or was it Lille?), his work is still untranslated and virtually unknown outside the Gallic world (as Yale University is now called). Yet his project — the demystifying or, as he prefers to say, the desexing of the privileging of fornication, both as act and metaphor, within the French philosophical circles — remains for me, and I trust others, the one decisive step that has been taken beyond the *cul de sac* or, in French, the *impasse* of Deconstruction. Briefly it advances the idea of the death of the subject to include the notion of, as he puts it, the philosopher or researcher 'him/her non-self'. 'Intellectual endeavour', explains Mensonge, 'has long been based on the false sexual paradigm, in its desire to lay bare, and then fill, the thing as it is. But philosophy must tell us that there is no thing to lay bare, no space to fill. In actuality, of course, the thing cannot be, for there is no actuality for it to be, or for that matter, not be, in' (all translations are, of course, my own). Mensonge's basic conclusion — which I take to be that there can be no philosophical object of attention whatsoever, since there is no philosophical subject to do the asking — seems to me one of the most potent conclusions of contemporary thought, and, when considered, quite inevitable. And his book, as I remarked in my article on it (it was published in the *Observer* last April 1), can truly be called seminal. Or at least it could have been, until it appeared.

I assume then it is my interest in Mensonge (to whom my university has just awarded an honorary degree, taken, needless to say, *in absentia*) that led to this auspicious invitation to address you on French literary theory and its impact, though the notion that literary theory has any impact on anyone whatsoever is one I have always found testing. But impact *where*? Conceivably (another word that, since Mensonge, cannot really be used) I should address you on the effect of the post-existentialist French philosophical theories in linguistics, sociology, history and literary hermeneutics on the academic community of which I am nowadays but a part-time member. For I take it, it is this impact I observe as I see my colleagues holding classes around the number-plates of cars, or running films backward in almost every seminar room I pass. But, equally conceivably, I could reflect on the impact of those same theories on the literary world of which I am also but a part-time member, and especially on the practice of writers and their writing. Here I should have to confess that, when at literary cocktail parties I seek to detain my fellow writers and discuss with them the latest article in *Glyph* on the floating signifier in *For Whom the Bell Tolls,* they mostly look at me strangely and begin to talk about the newest literary movement and who is in it and who is not. You might be pleased to learn that the newest movement in London is called VAT registered authors. Or should I talk about both, and the intersection of, the relationship, between the two? I think I will, but first...

First I would like to say that, despite all my remarks so far, I do happen to regard the analytical tendencies about which we are talking here as the major thought-movement of the west of the last 20 years, and the logical outcome of the direction of post-Romantic philosophy. Structuralism and Deconstruction do seem to me to contain a primary essential analysis of intellectual practice and of the philosophical impasse of contemporary culture, and they represent to us both its epistemological barrenness and its vital strength. Its concern for language and sign has massive implications for every form of cultural action and writerly exchange, and its leading figures — Levi-Strauss, Barthes, Foucault, Lacan, Derrida — have a power of creative achievement rare in our time. I also happen to distrust many of the practical implications that may be drawn from its theory, in pedagogy and in systematic research applications; I find many of the neophytes narrow, and the initial acts of originality are all too easily moved into barren and repetitious analytical tropes. In short, Deconstruction offers us not so much a mode of argument but a mode of self-knowledge, and its status is much that its originators themselves claim for it, as a set of original acts of writing. In this sense my earlier division should fall down, for it is precisely part of its proposal that the practice of theory and the practice of writing are not distinct. The practice of writing *is* the practice of criticism; and the practice of criticism the practice of writing. This suggests an ideal of the interfusion of the philosophical and the imaginative, the critical and the creative, which is perhaps the best derivation from the entire episode. In these terms we have within the tendency a potential reconciling and invigorating process, and this, to some degree, is what has happened in France, where the theory of a Barthes or a Derrida, inseparable from its discourse, is presented with the irreducible imaginative authority of any work of art. Or, we might say, the irreducible authority that *was* attached to any work of art, until it was subjected to Deconstructive practice.

Well, has there been any real impact from Structuralism over the last 20 years on British literary theory, and British literary practice? I propose to consider this matter autobiographically, with what remains of a self or an extant subject. My own academic study of literature began some 30 years ago, and at a time when the field was moving away from a predominantly historical, biographical and impressionistic approach to writers and writing, and beginning to assimilate the notions of the New Criticism and what used to be called Practical Criticism. In the ideas here compounded there was a significant derivation from Russian Formalism, from Modernist theory as formulated by Pound and Eliot, from Imagism and that revolt against the discursive that had marked so much modern writing, and from those developments of linguistic study that had been established in critical practice by Richards and Empson. But the dominant figure of the times was F.R. Leavis, whose own intellectual origins were interesting and complex. We should never forget how indebted Leavis was to the work of Eliot, Pound and the Modernists, but into their vision or approach he sought to integrate a cultural concern of a quite different order, an Arnoldian preoccupation with cultural values as critique of society. His own direct lineage of indebtedness went back, as he increasingly insisted, to D.H. Lawrence. And modernist and formalist critical lore were assimilated into a sense of pedagogic moral urgency which made the study of literature into a search for vital standards of living. The texts he studies were never simply discursive, but morally active. Appropriately, his approach was shaped at once by an internationalist intellectual history and an urgent, nativised provincialism, a special Britishness that was unmistakable in all he said and did. His Great Tradition of the novel thus incorporated international figures like Henry James and Joseph Conrad;

yet, peculiarly, they emerged as elements of our national literary history and its long-studied preoccupations. He rarely granted writers a purely philosophical or an aesthetic location, and he was averse to any criticism that inclined to read them in that way. His response to the literary achievement of his own contemporaries was often severely judging and cruelly narrow, not just because of the careful organization of his body of sympathies and literary expectations, but because he could not grant to the wasted culture he saw around him the simple potentiality of creating a great or even a genuinely important writer.

In retrospect, it seems to me that, despite that narrowness, Leavis had an extraordinary and significant impact on writers; he was the most determined and interesting critic about, and he said things that writers could use. In the postwar period British writers, especially novelists, were seeking to assess the potential of the tradition for present use, and Leavis gave them what looked like a usable past; writer after writer intertextualized, as we should now say, the tradition that Leavis made canonical. In so doing, they assimilated and re-presented the provinicialised values that Leavis celebrated, and the prevailing attempt of writers to get behind Modernism and return to the social and moral realist novel was greatly guided by him. Leavis in short provided a good deal of the covert theory behind the British novel of the 1950s, though that fact held no great interest for him; his interests were largely pedagogic and directed at the reformation of an irreformable culture. But what is clear is that, just as the provincial realist novel in Britain was itself to give ground in due course to broader and more various conceptions of fiction, so Leavis's own influence as critic and theoretician gave way, and for similar grounds.

So, by the Sixties, as critical theory came under increased pressure from linguistics and post-existential philosophies, from hermeneutics and semiology, his work was, one might say, largely dis-Kermoded if not totally dis-Lodged. Many critical approaches canvassed for the vacancy, and it soon became apparent that in schools and universities Leavis's great achievement had been to give literary study an urgency of purpose which, once lost, was impossible to recover. This then was the situation in which the arguments of Structuralism and Late Marxism entered English Departments which were themselves revising their syllabuses and ideology under the pressure of university expansion and the widening of structures of study. It was now that a good many younger figures began to nail their flag to the Structuralist mast, though very often in the interests of advancing the linguistic study of literature, or developing broader forms of cultural study in which questions of canons and traditions gave way to greater eclecticism; plurality of content encouraged systematization of theory. Literary criticism in universities needed, after all, to grow theoretical and professionalized, for so many were coming into the profession; criticism was for tenure. Out of this climate there emerged a body of literary theory, pure and applied, quite inconceivable in the moral urgency and philosophical pragmatism of the 1950s. It has done much: alerted us to the complex existence of discourse and sign, to the new grammatology, to the nature of literary production and consumption, to narrative theory. It has challenged our literary notions of the present and the real, and required of trained readers and perhaps trained writers the kinds of epistemological awareness that eluded both in the 1950s. All this has had potentially vital theoretical and creative results. Alas, it has also led to an increased detachment between the critical and the creative, as criticism has grown abstruse and often phenomenological in its study of verbal and semiotic events, and writers seeking from critics the one quality they have usually turned to them for, namely judgement, have been disappointed.

But has this new age of theory had any impact on the practice of Fiction, comparable even with that I associate with the era of Leavis? There can be no doubt at all we have seen a substantial change in the habits and practice of fiction in Britain — one generally happy result of which is that it no longer seems right to call much of it British, if this means an allegiance to the national tradition and the usable past. Where in the Fifties it was from a very real canal bank near Wakefield that all true art sprang, it now springs largely from some degree of awareness that reality is a constituted thing and not a given. By the 1960s the practices of the French *nouveau roman* and American Postmodernism (which were themselves largely directed by those two only honorary American experimentalists, Borges and Nabokov) began to make their modest mark even here. Certainly there seemed

to be something irreducibly *there* about the traditionally
British novel, so that frequently its frame stayed, even as its
contents were dismantled, as I believe they are in such books
as *The Golden Notebook, The French Lieutenant's Woman*
or even Paul Scott's *Raj Quartet*, but the trace of postmod-
ernist ideas was there. By the 1970s this dissolution in serious
fiction had, I believe, increased greatly, and it was invigo-
rated both by the feminist and the extraterritorial challenge
to British fiction, as it became clear that the English-language
novel, thanks to the spread of the English-language, func-
tioned over a global map. That period of new expansion
might well be dying now, but it has fundamentally transformed the character of the contemporary British novel.

So both in the academy and in the practice of fiction there
have been significant changes over the last 20 years, and they
seem to have something to do with the impact of French
ideals and those forces we loosely associate with Structuralism. But if we look more deeply, and ask whether these
changes actually reveal some deep change in the character of
British culture and ideology, I doubt very much if they do. I
have just received a letter from a young scholar-critic I
admire, working in one of our ancient universities. He has
been writing about a well-known, living British writer who,
as so often happens, is living in France. The letter begins:

> X [the name of the writer] has ruined me. Because he is not
> respected my work about him has received the same treat-
> ment. I have been slung out of all the Senior Common Rooms
> where his name and mine were linked. Truth to say, however
> and moreover, Y [another author he works on, but an early
> Modernist] earns a few boos and sneers too. But at least he's
> dead and a CLASSIC...

I mention this because it would not do for me to suggest that
today in this country there is much real intimacy, whether of
mind or body, between those who practice criticism and
those who write fiction, poetry or drama. The territories
may have parallel concerns, but they are distinct. Our critics
today are salaried professionals on campus, our writers live
in country rectories, fantasizing about strange sexual coup-
lings, or in Islington, where they do much the same, and the
twain meet rarely; and most academic departments of English do indeed still regard the term 'living writer' as a

contradiction. Debates over literary theory in the academy have had only indirect rather than direct impact on writing, and Britain still has no active literary-aesthetic discourse supporting its creative arts, or any really active contact bringing together academic critics and actual writers. The question then arises whether the effect of Structuralist influence here *could* bring about this, to me, desirable intimacy. Certainly it has not done so here in Britain. Theory lives *here*, on campus; writing lives *there*, largely in the marketplace. Writing functions in constant existential and cultural anxiety; criticism seems to have used theory to stabilize and professionalize itself into security. Indeed in many ways it has helped the critic to free himself from his traditional dependence upon the writer, by affording the prospect that literary study may become a system, an epistemology, a true science. In this world the literary text, if we accept that there *is* a literary text, is a socio-psycho-culturo-linguistico-ideological event, arising from an implied author, transacted by an enabling theory of literary production to an implied reader. It arises from the available generic and narratological variables intersecting with mentality or periodicity, in the form of a guilty contrivance, seeking by narrative cunning to exculpate itself through the devious logic of elusively signifying episodes. But the guilt can never be exculpated, the deed never forgiven; at the end of the construction there lies in wait the inevitable deconstructionist. Meanwhile, back there in small wooden sheds, there sit, typing, the guilty parties who create these self-falsifying paradigms, a logocentric proletariat that seeks to imply itself into existence. These persons we call writers, and they shall not escape.

I would like to believe the following: that art is an essential and fundamental mode of human enquiry, and that it is historically located in the culture and the discourse of its time; that hence we must live in a late twentieth-century age of style which in some fashion our arts are realizing. There is, to use a prevailing word a late twentieth century episteme: and it seems right to believe that recent French theory has laid bare many of its implications and significations. I would also like to think that, by whatever forms of intuition or aesthetic self-knowledge, our best writers, the writers we in the end must take seriously, have apprehended this, and are exploring the imaginative, the psychic, the perceptual, the linguistic form of our own historical presence. I would want to believe that it is from such realizations that the true history of mind, form and style is made; and that hence those who theorize and those who create share together a mode of apprehension, a common hunger to realize a contemporary fiction. But this I do not see. As a writer, I find myself, in relation to contemporary theory, in much the same condition that George Orwell, in 'Inside the Whale', found the modern writer — ragingly passive under the power of exterior structures he cannot reproduce and cannot control. This is a condition that Structuralism has interpreted often to us; and yet, as theory, Structuralism has become part of the onerous structure itself. The result is ambiguity, an ambiguity that as a writer, I read on my own page — where, in the end, the theoretics do not so much construct the imagination as become the web from which it must escape. In my own last book, *Rates of Exchange*, I found myself reflecting much on this matter. It was an ambiguity, a quarrel, an unease I tried to signify, not least in one of the epigraphs to the novel, on which I would like to end. It comes from that classic Lacanian text, *The Purloined Letter*, the actual author, if there are still to be actual authors, of which was Edgar Allan Poe. The quotation reads (let it dwell in the air):

'You have a quarrel on hand, I see,' said I, 'with some of the algebraists of Paris; but proceed.'

Well, I suppose I have; and I will.

WHAT HAVE THEY DONE TO US? THE THEORY MONSTER AND THE WRITER
Jacques Roubaud

My first words are words of apology: although I can read English and I usually read nothing but English, I have had few opportunities to speak English and as a writer, I write in French. Mine is a kind of Frenchglish contribution with paragraphs in English interspersed occasionally with bursts of untranslated French. It could be compared with the Welsh weather forecast: long periods of rain will be interrupted by short periods of showers.

The question under consideration is 'who has been doing what and to whom? And who exactly are *they* and who exactly are *us*'? My answer is that of one who writes poems and is a professional mathematician. It is necessarily partial, biased and idosyncratic. This statement is another apology.

I shall tackle the question 'who are they?' first. I will simplify it drastically: the 'French Literary Theorists' will be represented as being only one person, *une personne unique,* and for the moment I shall exclude from their ranks the deconstuctionists.

My moral portrait of this generic French Literary Theorist or FLT — a persona in the Poundian sense — is helped by Mrs. Sapsea's epitaph. Mrs. Sapsea's epitaph was prepared by her husband, Mr. Sapsea, and both, as you know, are characters in Charles Dickens' *The Mystery of Edwin Drood.*

Ethelinda
reverential wife of
Mr THOMAS SAPSEA
auctioneer, valuer, estate agent, etc...
of this city.
Whose knowledge of the world,
though somewhat extensive,

never brought him acquainted with
a SPIRIT
more capable of
looking up to him.
STRANGER PAUSE
and ask thyself the question,
CANST THOU DO LIKEWISE
if not,
with a blush retire.

The FLT is a monster, a chimera, an amphibious 'tarasque', a 'beast in the jungle', a *'bête glatissant'* like those found in the medieval French romances. It has the kind eyes of a ewe, the ears and shout of a fox, and forty whelps are barking inside its belly.

Or so, in the sixties and seventies in France, did the Theory of Literature appear to the respectful and bashful eyes of French writers, both poets and novelists.

To the conception of this monster contributed in unequal proportions structuralist linguistics, as exemplified by the godlike names of Saussure and Jakobson (we could add a late whiff of Chomskian generative and transformtional grammar); a few species of semiology and semiotics (Barthes, Greimas, Kristeva); some orthodox Freudian psychoanalysis, gradually and increasingly growing Lacanian; and countless varieties of Marxism, from Althusser to the gospel of Chairman Mao.

I will not speak here of the theories or pseudo-theories involved, as such. The debate on their consistency and relevance played practically no role at all in the way they were received, glorified and eventually influenced literature. Controversies, or learned discussions between specialists were warped beyond recognition. From the mouth of the monster only slogans issued: 'All is language!' 'Death to the author!' *'Vive le signifiant!' 'Revolution du language poétique!'* 'Writers are capitalists of meaning!' The insult of 'capitalist of knowledge' has been heaped repeatedly on teachers and scientists alike, as Jean-Claude Milner has shown in his recent book, *De l'école.*

Thus writers were confronted with a kind of 'theory-monster', were requested to adore it as a whole, or as a sum of independent parts, or as a sum of contrary parts, some good, some evil. Literature, in the last instance, was said to be merely 'language' oe *'l'inconscient'* or 'text' or 'intertextuality'. Writers were asked to forget the old ways, to modify their craft, to write differently in order to conform to the new rules.

We can well ask ourselves, how did it come to this? I will underline only two main features of a possible answer. First, placing theory in the foreground of any discussion of literary problems was not due to specialists in any of the fields involved. It was the stategy chosen by those who proclaimed themselves as the *new literary vanguard*. Their motto was — and I shall say it in French — *'Ote toi de là que je m'y mette!'* A wild west equivalent would be, 'Clear the range, cowboy!' Writers who had recourse to the 'appropriate' sort of conceptual machinery, remarkably effective in the short term, wanted to get rid of those who were unduly, to their eyes, present on the literary scene. They wanted to be the only ones there. I am not questioning that ambition, which could be considered legitimate. But who were to be their victims? I shall name only a few: the Surrealists, the engagé writers (either Sartrian or Stalinist), the nouveau roman. I am referring here, of course, to the 1960s generation, especially the *Tel Quel* group, who waved the banner of the avant-garde with the greatest decisiveness, intolerance and vociferousness.

Their strategy was similar to one used by other French literary groups since the Renaissance. The Pléiade, the classicists, the romantics used it, as did the Surrealists themselves. Further parallels could probably be drawn: they form a kind of constant in French cultural history since the 1550s. After the libertarian or political injunction, which followed the religious injunction, came the theoretical injunction, *l'injonction théorique*.

If we want to understand the success such an injunction has met with, at least for a time, it is important to emphasize the power and incompetence of the French press, particularly in the intellectual field. The age of *'l'universel reportage'* foreseen by Mallarmé, reached its climax precisely during those years. One does not know whether it is now proceeding towards something worse or only something different.

Journalistic commentary and relay was indispensable for the propagation of the theory-fashion, inseparable from the campaign launched by the avant-garde. Without it, it would have had no hope of success.

Before broaching the subject of 'what literary theory did to us', the writers, I should like to point out a paradoxical effect of the avant-garde's strategy, which I personally find rather entertaining. Let us take the Surrealists — who were more or less consciously the model of the vanguardists — as a point of comparison. The Surrealists selected out a limited number of writers from the past and they opposed these to those they wanted to get rid of. They drew up their famous lists: *'lire/ne pas lire'*. They also resorted to authorities taken from outside the field of literature — Marx or Freud. But they never ran the risk of having others than those who were writers (that is, themselves) put in their place. They never had to fear that *écrivants* would step into the shoes of *écrivains*. But this is precisely what happened in those years of the triumphant avant-garde. We have witnessed the paradox of that situation: a Barthes considered as the model of the *grand écrivain* (one must not forget that Artaud, Bataille and Joyce were dead and thus not dangerous). This means that, whatever judgement one wished to pass on the theoretical worth of Barthes' works, an obsolete, a *vieillotte* prose style was held up as the standard of modernity.

Let us come to the 'us' part. Among that protean throng called 'us', let us isolate a first group: those who flung the 'theory of literature' at the heads of other writers. The first question in that case becomes, 'what have they done to themselves?'. The answer is obvious: not much good, I fear. And above all, not much good to those who started writing at that time and believed in all good faith that one had to give in to the injunction of theory. A huge part of what was then written could have been written by some 20th century *précieuses ridicules*. What strikes one, above all, is the tedious illegibility of the writing, in no way, alas, a fertile difficulty, but a barenness due to misconception and ignorance. I am not the only one to think that one only writes by continuing other writings: it is hazardous to limit oneself to one or two 'masters', even worse if these be masters of theory and not writers.

If we now look at other writers, those who were not directly involved in the predominant vanguardist adventure, I think another distinction needs to be made. It is a very old one, but still in my eyes, effective: some write narrative prose, others write poetry. the novelists who were already writing at the time when the vanguardists reached their apogee, at least the best among them — Nathalie Sarraute, Claude Simon, Claude Ollier, went their own way. Let them be thanked for it. Those who started writing at that time were in a more difficult position. Georges Perec in his *Quel petit velo à guidon chromé au fond de la cour* made use of a course on rhetoric by Roland Barthes. Queneau's *Vol d'Icare* is a thematically 'modernist' novel; Calvino's *Se una notte d'inverno un viagiatore* is constructed using the *carrés sémantiques* of Greimas. But in each case, the use of concepts and methods from literary theory has been transmuted in the flesh and blood of an inventive prose by the presence of an ironical dimension which has been conspicuously absent in the productions of the 'vanguard' (with the exception of the poet Denis Roche). This could be the reason why there is a world of difference between the newspaper novel of Philippe Sollers, *Femmes,* a kind of new-wave Barbara Cartland, and Umberto Eco's *The Name of the Rose.*

My choice of Perec, Queneau, Calvino and Eco is not innocent. It points to another use of theory than the one that has been promoted by French Literary Theory. But as one says in stories, *'ceci est une autre histoire'*. As for the novelists who started writing later, the question does not arise for the theory monster has now disappeared.

What about the poets? Poets have more or less escaped the theory atom bomb for two reasons. The contingent one is that poets are not a journalistic commodity. This is not to be lauded, but at times it can be advantageous. The main reason is that the theoretical injunction was based on a kind of compound theory of literature with ingredients taken from one or another kind of linguistics. But poets have at all times and spontaneously thought that language — and particularly their own language — was their own private business. The relation between poets and their language has always been one of love. They guard their language jealously and therefore they have consistently ignored or rejected or paid lipservice to or misunderstood grammarians, rhetoricians, literary theorists and linguistics. This is as it should be.

For this reason the influence of French Literary Theorists on poets and poetry has been and still is non-existent. Poets have always used and go on using whatever materials of language that they can find: other poems, narrations, lists of things or events, aphorisms stolen from Wittgenstein, accounts of rugby tournaments in Cardiff, and, why not, texts written by linguists. As our great grandfather used to say:

> And as imagination bodies forth
> The forms of things unknown, the poet's pen
> Turns them to shapes, and gives to airy nothing
> A local habitation and a name.

Finally, a word about the deconstructionists. As a literary theory, I do not think it need be excepted from the rejection I mentioned by poets as a direct influence. But the origin of this theory, as one knows, is philosophical. It is a well-known and ancient truth that poetry and philosophy have an old and deep alliance. The recent renewal of French philosophy as well as the less pedestrian branches of Anglo-Saxon analytical philosophy, and above all Wittgenstein, have had and I think will go on having a beneficient influence on French poetry.

ROLAND BARTHES AND AFTER
Terry Eagleton

Whenever one witnesses an intensive outbreak of theory, of the kind that we have seen in literary studies for the past twenty years, one can be fairly sure that something is badly awry. I don't mean by this what David Holbrook or Denis Donoghue would be likely to mean by it — that such theory is itself the sign of some intellectual sickness or arid self-indulgence. I mean rather that rapid proliferations of theory tend to arise in historical situations where, for one reason or another, certain traditional intellectual practices have come unstuck. When this happens, when the customary rationales for such practices break down or become discredited, those practices are then forced into new kinds of self-reflectiveness. In one sense, 'theory' goes on all the time; in another sense, it speeds up dramatically at points where intellectual institutions enter upon a period of crisis. In such a situation, the latently sustaining assumptions of those institutions become for the first time *objectifiable;* they are 'de-naturalised', to become themselves possible objects of contention rather than the taken-for-granted frame within which particular contentions are conducted. Since no practice or institution can run smoothly while its supportive criteria of successful performance are themselves under interrogation, 'theory' and 'crisis' are logical bedfellows. Theory, in short, tends to break out with peculiar virulence when we are no longer sure what it is we are doing. It can then be deployed in one of two opposed political directions: either to refurbish a failing practice, supplying it with a renewed set of goals and rationales; or to put the skids under it entirely and suggest that an entirely different way of behaving is now on the historical agenda. Theory happens when it is both possible and necessary for it to do so. It does not come about simply because a number of exceptional individuals have dreamt up a number of original ideas.

The current explosion of cultural theory really dates from

the late 1960s, when the classical rationales of the 'humanities', and the academic institutions more generally, became the focus of unusually intensive debate in conditions of pervasive political turbulence. What happened was that liberal humanism, for long — and arguably still — the dominant ratifying ideology of cultural studies, was progressively discredited. There were all kinds of reasons for this, but one important one relates to the markedly contradictory relation of liberal humanism to late capitalism as a whole. Put briefly, liberal humanism is in one way a plausible, productive ideology for that society, and in another way, as the notion of an autonomous, unified, self-generative subject is shattered by postmodernism on the one hand and monopoly capital on the other, quite staggeringly implausible. Such an ideology, in the 1960s, was simply failing to answer to enough aspects of lived experience. It had become a hallmark for the relentless depoliticisation of culture, as it is still a code for such an operation today.

A few hours after I gave this talk at the ICA (of which this is a 'written' version), I was in Nottingham talking to about fifty schoolteachers of English, all working in the state system. One of the first things they did was to take me aside and save me a lot of tedious spadework by reminding me that there was no need to convince *them* that liberal humanism would not do (as there was, it seemed to me, with the ICA audience). Just try it on in the classroom, they suggested. It doesn't *work*. It doesn't fool anybody at all. It was perfectly clear to them that unless a political alternative to this deeply political version of literary studies was made available, they were wasting their time. They did not complain, as did various members of the ICA audience, that all this literary theory contained some dreadfully hard words — that Barthes did not speak in the language of Belgravia. Leave it to us, they suggested, to translate it into classroom practice.

Thames Television's 'English' programmes, on which I am an advisor, and which is intended for schoolchildren studying English, recently put out a brochure for its last series of programmes. On the cover were various photographs: a young woman in futuristic headgear, a white man and a black child, a mixed race group and so on. One of the foremost exponents of Leavisian liberal humanism in Britain, whose work is fairly influential on what goes on in English schools, wrote that it was perfectly clear from one glance at this cover that the programmes would not concern 'human relationships'. He also remarked that the 'English' programme was now clearly in the hands of the KGB. It is a timely reminder for those who think that liberal humanism is a straw target, 'theory' having swept all before it. It is of absolute importance that, in the classrooms of this society, human relationships are perceived as genderless, classless and white.

'Literature' in this society has now become a refuge for those who have long since given up trying to locate value elsewhere. This is why the contention over the meaning of literature is political to its roots. For what people fear they are being deprived of is not just one area of fundamental value but, in a society where broader political options seemed increasingly to shut down as the euphoric 60s rolled into the crisis-ridden 70s and 80s, nothing less than the sole surviving enclave of value *as such.* If the materialists and post-structuralists can get their grubby hands even on *that,* then the game is well and truly up. This is why 'literature', that enduring reserve of human generosity and nobility of spirit, is defended with all the viciousness and visceral anxiety of a cultural bourgeoisie who have long since ceased to find freedom, spiritual depth and creativity anywhere outside George Eliot.

In this context, the importance of Roland Barthes becomes clear. For it is surely the case that, after Barthes and his fellow theorists, literature and literary criticism are no longer possible. For the early Barthes of *Writing Degree Zero,* literature is an institution quite inseparable from a class-division of languages, a gesture of exclusion, separation and repression. The early, para-Marxian Barthes still believes, with Walter Benjamin, that 'every document of civilisation is at the same time a record of barbarism'. How then can there be a literary critical discourse which escapes the complicity and contamination which for Barthes is the very condition of a separated 'literary' language? The only 'authentic' literature in such political conditions is one which proclaims and testifies to its own impossibility. This, of course, is the moment of modernism, and with Barthes and Derrida the moment where such modernism drifts to take root in 'theory' itself, where it becomes possible for the first time after Benjamin and Adorno to speak not just of a theory of modernism but of a distinctively modernist theory. The only exit from the ineluctable social guilt of the literary institution would seem to be a writing which enunciates and undercuts itself in a single gesture — a discourse of irony and *aporia,* an 'abysmal' intertwining of commitment and withdrawal, affirmation and denial, which might then constitute, as *'écriture'* or 'textuality', a kind of guerilla tactics within academia, distinguishable from that institution not by its claim to some higher metaphysical authenticity but merely by the peculiarly acrobatic self-reflexiveness with which it manages ceaselessly to name its own ideological guilt.

The irony, then, is that there was surely no more celebrated French institution than Roland Barthes. 'Roland Barthes, and other Mythologies', runs the title of an essay by Wole Soyinka. But this is not just the old narrative of 'incorporation', for the whole dialectical irony of such modernism is to know itself as always already in part incorporated from the outset, inscribing within itself its historically inevitable collusiveness with what it nonetheless never ceases to wage war against. Cultural modernism is not merely contemporaneous with mass culture but in part an effect of it: in resisting its own dreary reduction to commodity status, the typical modernist artefact lays claim to a mysterious autonomy which, exactly, reproduces one characteristic structure of the commodity itself. What escapes is then 'style' or pleasure, that utopian undertow which can never be precisely formalised within the structures of exchange.

If the modernist enterprise of *Writing Degree Zero* cannot in the end give the slip to the deadweight of History, then a turn towards 'postmodernism' is always tempting. This is the Barthes of *Mythologies* and *Système de la Mode,* who will scandalise the academic bourgeoisie not by his avantgarde anti-realism but by his craftily calculated 'descent' into that very different form of unrealism, late consumerist culture itself. Instead of holding out by the force of *écriture* against that degraded, libidinally decathected commodity culture, the Barthes of *Mythologies* will take it as his very raw material, slipping from aesthetics to 'everyday life' while reinforcing in that very gesture the supremely absorptive power of semiology, which is quite indifferent to the cultural status of its object. This project, too, has its emancipatory limits. For there is a sense in which you can only put bricks in the Tate once, if the subversive charge of that gesture is not to be dissipated. Barthes, accordingly, moved on, impelled by his very Sartrian horror of permitting the *pour-soi* to congeal into some lethally institutionalised *en-soi*, of permitting desire to be captivated by its arbitrary objects. Semiotics served its scandalising purpose in destabilising distinctions between 'high' and 'low' culture, but was itself, paradoxically, a stabilising system. Was a 'destabilising theory' itself an oxymoron? Both Balzac *and* steak and chips: perhaps this angers the academics only to the extent that it also consoles their hunger for system, sealing these ill-assorted objects within the same, easily academicised discourse.

The early Barthes sought to undermine traditional liberal humanism with its old bugbear science, remorselessly formalising texts, pokerfacedly pigeonholing the most apparently contingent of experiences. When this strategy threatens to become itself coded and contained as the academic discipline of 'structuralism', Barthes impudently thrusts it into reverse, seizing upon anything — pleasure, the body, the recesses of the private — which might be offered (foolishly and delusorily, in my view) as the 'other' of what has now become, in familiar late Frankfurt school style, a predictably seamless ideological monolith. Michel Foucault was at least more evasively inconsistent about how such libidinal surfaces might give the slip to power. Soon Barthes will end up repeating the ideology of liberal humanism in an anti-humanist idiom, headily celebrating the orgasmic force of the 'text' as — it would seem — the sole surviving enclave or oasis of emancipation. David Holbrook detests the idiom, but he might take the general point. What had become lost throughout the whole of this restlessly provisional process of eluding, and then self-eluding, was that moment of *political* modernism which the early Barthes, editor of a theatre journal, found signalled in the name of Brecht. Brecht could not of course be simply reinvented in the political conditions of post-war France, but he is, among other things, a powerful antidote to post-Marxist and post-structuralist pessimism, with its conviction that power is ubiquitous, desire insatiable, the Law absolute, meaning self-molesting, the ego impotent and derisory, global theories of society terroristic, communication inconceivable. All of that, in post-

structuralism, curiously blends with a sporadic euphoria —
jouissance, the thrills and spills of the skidding signifier —
which, so to speak, keeps the revolution warm at the level of
discourse.

Barthes's problem was that, failing to reinvent Brecht, he
became instead an Azdak — rogue, scavenger, opportunist
and *bricoleur,* the burr on the ass of the Establishment. If this
richly challenged bourgeois institutions, generating a whole
gamut of concepts we can still gratefully put to use, it also in
its own way re-enacted the ever-changing fashions of late
capitalist consumerism. The point of the political avant garde
is that it *combines* two moments which are in Barthes really
chronologically separated: the ironic, critical, negating force
of 'high' modernism, and the insistence on the integration of
art and social practice which is parodied in the soup cans of
postmodernism. Once that crucial moment is lost, once the
revolutionary avant-garde tradition is surrendered, the
oppositional intellectual veers between a mere dissociative
ironising on the one hand, and an *ersatz* deconstruction of
'art' and 'life' on the other. It is surely not difficult to see the
strengths and limits of a Barthes as the strengths and limits of
any radical intellectual in transition from the discredited
shibboleths of liberal humanism to the construction of a
revolutionary culture. Barthes did not live to see the latter,
and by the end would very probably have been little ena-
moured of it if he had; but he served to keep that revolution
warm, and to invent for it new guerilla tactics and fragments
of subversive strategies for which we are enduringly in his
debt.

THE FEMINIST POLITICS OF LITERARY THEORY
Cora Kaplan

About ten years ago, durig the high point of feminist activ-
ism in Britain you could find a new-minted piece of folk
wisdom inscribed n the walls of women's loos throughout
the country, and quoted endlessly in the literature of the
movment: 'A Woman Without a Man is Like a Fish Without
a Bicycle'. As a defiant slogan of independence and autonomy it has always irritated me, not only for its 'separatist'
implications or its disturbing, Dali-esque juxtaposition of
selves and things, but also for its complacent essentialism and
the false (in-) congruities of its metaphor. Women aren't like
fish, supplied with a natural element and equipped for easy
passage through it. The 'revolutionary' choice for them will
never be for a streamlined new identity in harmony with an
environment in which rust-prone, male-designed transport
technology is redunndant. At many points in the ICA
weekend 'Crossing the Channel' as writers and critics
proudly maintained the uselessness of 'theory' for their practices, and as several of them disavowed both the present and
historical connection between literature and politics, I found
my least favourite feminist epigram swimming into view
suitably revamped for the occasion — 'A critic without a
theory of representation is like ... a writer without a politics
is like....'

The aesthetic, as either art practice or as commentary, was
slowly glassed in, a lonely fish in a pure element, safe from
that wobbly, effortful journey through twentieth century
terrains of catastrophe and contradiction that some of us had
thought was the point and process both of writing and
reading. 'Theory', which I hardly recognised in the alienated
and reified form in which the term was used by both French
and English participants, had been for me, and, I know, for
many other feminist readers, writers and cultural critics a
way of understanding that grim and comic conjunction of
self 'in' and 'out' of society that the literary inscribes, by

offering us both a theory of representation and of gender as constructed rather than natural meanings.

As the weekend wore on I could see other feminists in the audience (which was, as is usual at cultural events, at least half female while the platform sported only two women) becoming more and more restive. It wasn't simply that they were disturbed by the neo-neo-formalism of so many of the contributions which privileged the 'writer' and 'critic' as men of genius (Let's face it, Frank Kermode had said in a related event some few weeks before, There are a few really great critics and everyone knows who they are.), whose best work must be above the heads of and apart from the concerns of 'the masses'. It was that the negative history of the engagement between French theory and British and French literary practice being sketched out by most of the speakers bore no relationship to the realities of that engagement for women over the last fifteen years. Because gender was never introduced by any of the invited participants as a meaningful variable in the Anglo-French cultural development, and feminist theory or imaginative writing was barely mentioned, large and significant chunks of the cultural history of the past couple of decades were simply omitted from the discussion.

For the engagement of feminism with 'theory' in France, Britain and the United States has had a major impact on writing and criticism both inside and outside academia, and has been one of the main forces which has kept French structuralist, psychoanalytic, linguistic and political analysis from being wholly denatured and depoliticised as it crossed various waters.

Althusser, Lacan, Barthes, Derrida, Macherey, Foucault have been appropriated by English-speaking feminists as part of their analysis of sexual difference, of the persistence of femininity and of the crucial place of visual and written representation in the construction, maintenance and subversion of sexual ideologies. The critiques and innovations of French feminists, such as Luce Irigary, Michèle Montrelay, Hélène Cixous, Catherine Clément and the manifestos and texts of the new feminist avant-garde writers have had a relatively wide translation and circulation. Their work has contributed importantly to both an extension and critique of psychoanalytic theories of sexual difference. The work of

Julia Kristeva has been especially influential around questions of the relationship between subjectivity and writing. In particular Irigary and Monique Wittig have suggested to aspiring Anglophone feminist novelists and poets that imaginative writing can elide the space between a theory of difference and an art practice.

Literature, as a cultural object has a different place in feminist cutural and historical analysis than it does in androcentric criticism. One of the central historical discourses in which sexual difference is represented as both a social and psychic reality, it is also one of the few public genres in which women themselves spoke about these questions. For feminist critics, the literary is always already political in very obvious and common sense ways. For this reason, much feminist criticism of the late sixties and early seventies worked on literary texts by women as if they were 'true' accounts of the socially real, and on literary texts by men as if they were fantasies saturated with dominant and biased sexual meaning.

This 'common sense' approach to the literary, which did not have a theory of representation or of the specificity of imaginative writing, and which assumed a curious psychic separatism about the processes of writing by men and women was soon seen to be of somewhat limited use in understanding how sexual ideologies are constructed and circulated so that they assume 'natural' meaning for both men and women as writers and readers. Feminist critics began to look around for more adequate explanations of ideology, writing and sexual difference than were available through the liberal humanist approaches, or the new critical formalism in which most of them had been trained. While male critics in Britain had as a main spur to the development of marxist criticism the need to dismantle the hegemony of Leavisite notions of culture, and behind them, a conservative 19th-century romanticism, feminist critics, who were very much on the margins of the tertiary teaching of literature, though forming the majority of students of literature, were intervening to overthrow both these older humanisms and to critique the androcentric assumptions of the new male marxist critics. Literature, film, visual arts were central objects of feminist analysis of women's subordination. It was in these practices, together with the critical consensus that supported them and constructed their canons, that the languages and images through which subordinate female identities were constructed and naturalised could be identified. Moreover both the visual and written text demonstrate the connection between our fantasies of sexual difference (the psychic structure of difference) and its social meanings. Marxist literary criticism has always been somewhat nervous and tentative in its handling of the construction of social hierarchy in literary texts, as if class were only really meaningful as a lived relation, or an economic fact. Feminism on the contrary has insisted from Mary Wollstonecraft onwards that representations of sexual identity as well as its social articulation are both crucial elements in the subordination of women. It was Wollstonecraft, too, who identified the novel as the popular literary genre directed at women readers which would powerfully feed and reinforce denigrating, 'sentimental' definitions of femininity.

Both in the 19th century and today, feminism has seen the question of the representation of women, sexual difference, and gender relations as a 'political' question. Since the literary was one of the primary sites of that representation it could never, whatever its didactic purpose, wholly assume for the woman reader that universalising function which obscured the real relations of social hierarchy and difference. The 'stuff' of the literary, its narratives and its poetics, is steeped (one might say mired) in the contemplation and elaboration of sexual difference and inequalities — and this is as true of most imaginative writing by women as it is of most men's writing. Thus no feminist critic, writer or artist today could assert with the bland assurance of some of the men on the platform of 'Crossing the Channel' that art was the 'other' of politics, or that some knowledge of contemporary theories of the psyche and of language were not a useful part of the equipment of both writer or cultural critic.

Feminist inroads

I would like to argue that the feminist intervention into cultural practice has, in the last fifteen years, actually transformed dominant ideas about culture. It has made greater inroads on the notion of art as only good where it speaks for a general humanity than any cultural intervention excepting the renaissance of Black writing and art in the United States from the late fifties onwards. An inroad is by no means a victory, as any glance at the frequently spiteful and partisan reviews which feminist writing gets in newspaper and periodical press can easily confirm. But even the most mischievous and spiteful review points to an arena of public confrontation over these questions and usually reflects a more sophisticated form and language of debate over them than was around ten years ago

The ICA weekend, which so angered the feminists in the audience, revealed another sort of resistance to the combined intervention of specifically political cultural practice and the socialist and feminist criticism that supports it — a denial, a disavowal of the terms of that art practice, and a retreat to familiar positions of elitism and aestheticism. While women weren't mentioned, the 'crowd' as reader was despised, with only Salman Rushdie and Raphael Samuel to defend political art, politicised artists and the idea of a broad readership. (One of the best moments of the weekend occurred when one of the French participants, Serge Faucheraux, in a burst of post-lunch hyperbole, insisted that none of the hundreds of thousands of French people who followed Sartre's bier had read a word he had written, proof positive that the multitude were swinish illiterates, and left-wing writers, even when dead, dangerous demagogues. 'How do you know,' inquired Rushdie with bitter politeness, 'Did you ask them?') Women were, I guess, virtually included in this discussion, since feminism was one of the unarticulated targets of the defenders of formalist art. The question of theory was more difficult, since Rushdie together with other writers tended to see its uses in imaginative writing as marginal, pointing out that he took his models and examples from the popular storytellers still practising in the subcontinent.

Perhaps, in order to point out the specific uses of 'theory' for feminism in general and feminist criticism in particular I should also tell a story, one which places those uses in concrete historical example, rather than asserting a general influence. From 1976 until 1978, I was a member of a group called unaesthetically but accurately The Marxist-Feminist Literature Collective. When I joined, it had been going for some months, and its membership hovered around 12 for its

duration as a group. It was formed initially as a reading group
of feminists interested in developing a marxist-feminist
analysis of literature and most, though not quite all of the
members were students or teachers of literature in higher
education. We ranged in age from under twenty to over
forty, and there were always some Americans (either expatri-
ates like myself, or temporary members) among us. The
group met in London but its members came from all over the
bottom half of Britain, from Brighton, Oxford, Reading,
Birmingham and Bristol. Our early reading list contained
classical marxist writing on literature and French theory —
Barthes, Saussure, Macherey, Kristeva, Lacan and others.
We met quite often, every two or three weeks, and attend-
ance was regular. Our aim was first to understand the theory
we were reading, and it was interesting that even the most
professionally   experienced   members   of   the   group
approached the theoretical texts with some nervousness. It
was often the younger members who were initially most
confident in dealing with them. In the second place we
wanted to appropriate what we read for an analysis of literature that took account of both class and gender, but saw them
as separate and equal determinants. We were moderately
confident that we could integrate Marxism and feminism,
and some of us believed that we could also successfully
integrate psychoanalytic theory with both; but we were
aware from the beginning of the considerable difficulties of
such syntheses, and our discussions continued to raise new
problems to resolve.

I still have some of the papers from the group, especially
from the year 76-77 and it is clear we worked hard, regularly
writing and circulating short papers for discussion. At some
point we decided to offer a collective paper ('Women's Writing: *Jane Eyre, Shirley, Villette, Aurora Leigh, in 1848: The
Sociology of Literature*, Proceedings of the Essex University
Sociology of Literature Conference, 1977. Essex, 1978) to
the 1977 Sociology of Literature Conference at Essex (then
the only socialist lit-crit annual gathering) which took as its
topic the year 1848. We read, therefore, texts from that
period — the Brontes and Elizabeth Barrett Browning, and
tried out our tentative critical syntheses on these 19th-
century writings. A whole weekend was given up to putting
together the bits of the paper, editing sections down to size,

writing translations, agreeing the final copy. It was painful, time-consuming, humbling, instructive and exhilarating. Ten of us appeared at the conference and we gave the paper a dramatic performance, all of us reading parts of it out. Even at a conference of socialist literary critics, our presentation and the paper itself caused a mild sensation. Very few of the men at the conference had any experience of collective writing of an intellectual as opposed to an agit-prop political kind, and I suspect that we were challenging more than a male marxist hegemony around criticism and theory, but, equally important, the 'individualist' notion of criticism as the work of single intellects working alone, something that marxist critical practice as opposed to theory had not really confronted. Looking back too, I think the obvious differences in the group in terms of age and status was shocking, breaking down for a few minutes at least the institutional barriers between students and tutors, not in the 'acceptable' social way over a drink, but via a democratic, intellectual practice. (This was made easier because we were not students and teachers at the same institutions, but it did help to provide a better model for intra-institutional relations.)

That group was absolutely formative for my work. I had written one big piece of feminist criticism before I joined, but working on the conference paper confirmed my interest in the mid-19th century and dictated the intellectual course of my writing for many years after. My fear of theory as an alien and impenetrable discourse — something felt by many of us trained in the humanities — was permanently dissolved and my sense of its political uses, in analysing representation and relating that analysis to wider socialist and feminist questions was clarified and confirmed. The group continued for at least a year after the Essex event, with some changes in membership, and contributed in a collective way to other venues, though never as spectacularly.

Throughout the life of the group we debated the politics of accessibility and discussed the different ways of arguing the questions of culture and politics with which we were all concerned. Who were the audience we wished mainly to address? How could we talk to more women, and not only middle-class university educated white women. We discussed the ways in which it was appropriate to use our collective work to aid our careers which were at very different stages.

We learned a great deal about the contradictions and difficulties of working collectively in a field which prized the individual and original insight above any other, learning how hard it was to 'let go' of a private property in ideas and language. We did not entirely let go. Rather more of us are now working as lecturers in polytechnics and universities — many of the younger women are now in those jobs, but a few are working in further education and community projects. A good number of us, perhaps most of us, would still see ourselves as socialist-feminists, or at any rate, socialists and feminists. As well as changing the direction of our own writing, the collective experience was very important to me in thinking about the function of criticism in the seventies and eighties, and it is with these thoughts that I want to close this piece.

In recent male marxist criticism 'friendly' to feminism, it has become common to find in the women's movement of the last fifteen years and the cultural practice that has emerged from it a model for a revitalised, political, even revolutionary relationship between art and society. Terry Eagleton in both *Literary Theory* (1984) and in *The Function of Criticism* (1984) has made interesting points along these lines, and Francis Mulhern has also talked about the renaissance of the political novel in the utopian writing of American feminist writers, both black and white (*New Statesman*, 22 March 1985). I suppose I have been saying something like this myself in the above discussion, posing the intrinsically political and progressive nature of feminist cultural analysis against a resurgent reactionary aesthetic shared by too many of the writers and critics on the ICA platform on the weekend in question, but symptomatic of a larger movement to the right in the USA and Britain under Reagan and Thatcher, and the related shifts away from a left analysis of cultural practice in France in recent years.

It is important however not to idealize or reify the gains of the women's movement or its present effects around a cultural politics, for it, too, is dispersed and in many ways demoralised in all these countries. If its cultural interventions are still strong, their base in a social movement with a public profile and an agreed political agenda and strategy has significantly weakened. A cultural politics without a strong political culture behind it can only reminisce (note the increasing number of feminist autobiographies which have appeared in the last few years), and however powerful its literary voice it will not have an ongoing social movement to critique and encourage it. Without that critique, it can, like all cultural movements that outlive their immediate political moment, become smug, institutionalised, reflexive and stale. Cultural practice is rarely exactly in sync with the political moments that produce it, but equally they will not be part of a 'counterpublic sphere' (Eagleton's phrase) or a 'revolutionary literary culture' (Mulhern's) without them. It is one of those semi-tragic ironies that feminist criticism has become legitimate within the academy in Britain at a moment when education is contracting. There are no new jobs for the new feminist scholars which our graduate programs have produced, and while the disproportion between men and women in English studies continues to make it a 'women's subject' the demands of these women to be taught feminist texts and feminist forms of analysis cannot be met by existing faculty.

In the discussion which I chaired between Terry Eagleton and Frank Kermode the ostensible topic was the uses of French theory (Barthes in particular) for literary criticism. Kermode gave a pessimistic and depressed account of the influence or efficacy of such theory. He thought that there were few marxist critics teaching in institutions of higher learning in Britain, fewer still who were any good at it. Barthes' influence had been negligible, and Barthes' importance anyway was not as a radical thinker or theorist, but as an intellectual in a more elite and literary mode. Eagleton was optimistic, and looked to the spread of new ideas even to the secondary schools. He certainly asserted the vital connection between theory and politics, and saw a potential triumph of the new English teaching against an older reactionary humanism. In the way they spoke however I sensed a still shared notion of 'the critic' as a rather isolated academic figure (like older romantic notions of the writer). Kermode and Eagleton differed importantly on the question of text and canon, and on the possibility or desirability of politicising the teaching of literature in the academy.

What was missing from their discourse (though not I would have thought from their actual practice) was any notion of a dialectic relationship between critic-tutor and

students, a relationship which has been enormously important for feminist critics, for it is in and through their women
students that they have to a great extent developed and
expanded their critique of male-dominated culture. If a generation of students are coming into polytechnics and universities who have no experience of left social movements then
the role of tutor-critic shifts again. The agenda, reading lists
and discussions must be changed to give then an historical
grounding in the progressive literature and cultural analysis
they are still asking to study. The tutor/critic must engage
with their sense of the present political moment, not only his
or her own. The setting up of women's studies in the seventies and early eighties in higher and further education was a
most important development for it now provides a fragile
but still *in place* infrastructure for the development of new
political ideas.

Women are channelled into literary studies for all the
wrong reasons to do with reactionary and essentialist notions of female attributes and skills, but they also choose that
area quite consciously as one in which the psychic and social
aspects of sexuality, difference and gender relations will be
studied. It is no use trying to create an ideal model of cultural
intervention out of a social movement whose character has
changed with the changing times. But it is worth trying to
make sure that the eclipse of a feminist and socialist politics
does not take place, and that its continuing vitality in art
practice and cultural analysis be used to get young men and
women who have come to adulthood in the last six years to
begin to construct a progressive cultural politics for the
eighties. Time for us fish to get on our bikes.

THE ARCHAEOLOGY OF MICHEL FOUCAULT

MICHEL FOUCAULT: THE DEATH OF THE AUTHOR
Alan Sheridan

Michel Foucault died on 25 June 1984. He was fifty-seven. Forty-eight hours after his death, *Le Monde* devoted a large section of its front page and two more pages to the testimony of colleagues and friends. This — and the fact that the then Prime Minister felt it incumbent upon him to issue a statement — is suggestive of the awe in which France holds its leading intellectuals. And there can be no doubt that since the death of Sartre — and, in his case, the vogue of his work had perished some twenty years before the man — Foucault was France's leading intellectual. This would have been confirmed in a poll taken among, say, Foucault's colleagues at the Collège de France and was, in fact, confirmed in a public opinion poll taken some years ago. His books sold in numbers that were enjoyed only by the most popular novelists. They were translated into practically every language in which books are printed, though, with the usual exception of the Yugoslav languages and the temporary one of Polish, not in those of the socialist countries. Clearly, the exclusion of the socialist countries from Foucault's readership was based, among other things, on an assessment of his potential appeal: his books would sell not too few copies, but too many. Fortunately, commercial publishers respect the law of the market-place, which the Romans called the forum, and which was also the place where citizens could speak their minds. Intellectual freedom would seem to benefit more from the profit motive than from its abolition.

The notion of the death of the author has not removed interest in the circumstances of an author's death — or life. In any case, what was involved in the notion was a reinterpretation of what the term 'author' meant, rather than a seeking after anonymity. Certainly the notion of the founding subject was rejected, leaving the notion of author problematic, without centre and with shifting boundaries. It was no doubt necessary in the cultural context of the 1960s to reexamine the notion of author, to empty it of its plenitude, to see it rather as a relative, operational term that would refer to different degrees and different kinds of individuality depending on the type of discourse being used by the author and on the possibility for individual variation offered by the culture in which he works. But the notion of the 'death of the author' was taken by some to mean that it was somehow unprofessional to make any reference whatsoever to the individual who just happened to carry the same name as the author. It was even thought that there was something essentially un-Foucaldian in trying to see Foucault's work as a whole, as if any of his books could just as easily have been communicated by some different medium.

Such an attitude belongs to the extreme scientism of its time. It was as if the power generated by the repression of the individual self were poured into collective manifestations. It was a time when the scientism of certain Western intellectuals was perfectly compatible with mass hysteria or with group terrorism, providing they operated under the correct ideological labels; when, for many, the activities of the Red Guards in China or the Red Brigades in Italy represented an ideal of authentic action. It would not be true to say that Foucault was entirely unaffected by the flight from individualism: there was a time when he seemed to prefer the cameraderie of the popular assembly to the loneliness of the polling booth. But he resisted the lures of Leftism as he had abandoned, many years earlier, the illusions of bureaucratic socialism. Although he had a passionate interest in day-to-day political and social questions, he never joined any political party or group since his very brief membership of the Communist Party as a young man. It was not that he considered himself to be above the battle, but rather that he regarded each issue as a separate battle. He hated the automatic response that does one's thinking for one, the homogenization of disparate causes, the assumption, for example, that feminists, as such, should support CND, or gay men the miners — the pickets, that is, not those trying to get into work.

This taste for the individual, for the discrete runs right through Foucault's thinking. To begin with, and most obviously, his *oeuvre* is like no other. What is more, none of his books is like any other. He never wrote a single work that can be said to belong to the discipline in which he was trained and which he taught for many years. Yet he marched fearlessly into several others: psychiatry and medicine, art and literature, the social and political sciences, economics, biology, linguistics, penology and even subjects not usually taught in the universities, or even in polytechnics, like sexuality.

These heterogenous disciplines lay around the pages of his books promiscuously forming themselves into the most unexpected conjunctions. But he was not some kind of eccentric amateur, plundering other men's researches and producing a meta-discourse out of secondary sources. No, he actually worked harder and longer than most of the 'professionals' in each field. Directing all was the free play of an emancipated intelligence, exercising the imagination of a creative artist.

His whole oeuvre displays a sovereign contempt for what are called the 'sciences of man', for their scientific pretentions, their closed, self-validating systems, their regimes of truth. One characteristic of the truth-claiming discourse is its support-network. You may be what is called a sociologist, you hold a lectureship in sociology, you have time to read little else but books by fellow sociologists, you write articles for sociological journals. You spend your life trying desperately to say something new, but not so new as to lessen your chances of a Chair. You have to publish to get promoted, so you find a publisher's editor anxiously looking for bright young talent (his job depends on finding it). Neither you nor the publisher expects to make much money out of your book. You have a salary with tenure and the publisher is happy if the machine ticks over. Your book is published in hardback at £19.50. It is reviewed in sociological journals. It doesn't make the Sunday or daily papers, but it gets reviewed in *New Society* and the *THES*. It sells about 500 copies to the university and polytechnic libraries. A year later, your publisher binds the remaining sheets as a paperback, selling at £7.95, with a lurid cover depicting two bald-headed youths with safety-pins in their left ears — the book is called *The Sociology of Deviance*. The book appears on colleagues' reading-lists and is bought by students. The circle of mutual self-interest is complete and our sociologist of deviance continues in his totally undeviant way, safe in the arms of his support-network.

Foucault had no such support-network, no institutional validation for his books. In the early part of his career, he even chose exile as a cultural diplomat in preference to the academic life. He had to conquer his readership from zero: *L'Histoire de la folie* was even turned down by three leading Paris publishers. Eventually, Foucault returned to France and spent the next ten years teaching philosophy. But his books led a parallel existence to — and did not coincide with — his work as a university teacher. They did not emerge out of his lectures: there was no way a philosophy professor could lecture on 'the history of madness', 'the origins of clinical medicine', or the interlinked histories of biology, philology and political economy. It was not until he had his own Chair at the Collège de France, which is not, of course, a degree-giving university body, but a centre for public lectures, and was free to lecture on whatever he liked, that lecturing and writing became one. By that time he was a national figure and had conquered his public.

Foucault's legacy

What, then, did Foucault offer that public? Not a systematic view of the world, though I suspect that the reason for his success, for the attention he receives in the Academy, perhaps even for the size of his audience today, is to be found in that lusting after Truth — with a capital T — that is, of course, a respectable mask for the Will to Power. Certainty commands; uncertainty is brushed aside, or, if it takes the form of persistent questioning, it may either be tolerated or silenced, depending on the nature of the political regime. If Foucault's books do not tell us how to view the world, or how to act, what do they do? What are they? They are 'fictions', says Foucault. He is not saying, of course, that he has become a novelist. He is saying that in some crucial way his books are more like novels than they are like truth-claiming discourse. At their simplest, novels tell stories — in the sense in which children used to be punished for telling stories, that is lies.

For reasons that are better left mysterious, though there

are plenty of theorists offering to penetrate the mystery, we actually enjoy listening to these lies, knowing them to be lies, marvelling at the inventiveness of the liar. They offer us the freedom of alternative accounts. Yet such is the skill of the liar that we come to believe that the liar is telling the truth: we come under a sort of spell. Then the story ends: the spell is broken. It was all lies after all. Yet the best stories do not end there, they go on, working within us, subtly affecting our view of the world, actually increasing our capacity to enjoy the world. 'There's a lot of truth in what that liar said,' we say.

We don't put down *Ulysses* and say, 'Yes, Joyce is right, that is how the world is,' or alternatively, 'Joyce has got it wrong, the world isn't a bit like that.' Joyce's view doesn't conflict with Proust's, or Kafka's, though they were all writing at the same time. Novelists do, implicitly, offer views of the world, but they are non-exclusive ones. The views of the world offered in Foucault's books are of the same kind, which is why he has never indulged in polemics or felt the need to lay about supposed rivals before embarking on his latest hypothesis.

But in distinguishing himself from the truth-claiming practitioners of the human sciences, Foucault was also saying that no one mode of discourse has, in itself, a greater access to truth than any other, that all forms of discourse are 'fictions', that we can only see the world in terms of 'fictions'. If truth-claiming discourses do not help us to understand the world and ourselves any more than avowedly fictitious discourses, because their claim to truth is itself a fiction, then those discourses that acknowledge their fictitious nature are more likely to assist our understanding than those based on a lie. This confirms what most people, those unscarred by the Will to Truth, have always known: that a more profitable and pleasurable time is to be had with the poets and novelists, paywrights and film-makers, musicians and artists, than with the philosophers and theologians, the theorists of society and of the psyche, even cultural and literary theorists. How many of those theoreticians would one read, unless it were part of one's job to do so, unless one were defending an acquired position within the Truth from attack by a rival Truth, if one became convinced that Truth was not to be found in their books? How many would survive? Would

anyone bother to plough through the *Summa Theologica,*
The Phenomenology of Mind, Capital, The Critique of Di-
alectical Reason or Lacan's *Ecrits,* if, as I say, he or she did
not believe in its Truth or in the Truth of some rival account,
unless, in some sense, he or she were paid to do so? And they
are the peaks in their respective regions: what of the rest?

If Foucault's books are 'fictions', do they have anything in
common? In his introduction to *L'Usage des Plaisirs,* the
second volume of the *History of Sexuality,* published just
before his death, Foucault provides his own answer: they are
the products of a philosophical exercise. The purpose of that
exercise is 'to find out the extent to which the work of
thinking about one's own history, can free thought of what it
silently thinks and allow it to think otherwise.' His books are
directed, then, at those who are trying to free themselves
from the Will to Truth — which is why many who are
consumed by that lust, those who, in Foucault's words, use
philosophy to 'legitimate what they already know', find his
agnosticism such an irresistible challenge. But what replaces
one's Will to Truth? Why did Foucault go on writing and
why should we go on reading him? Again Foucault gives the
answer. My motive, he says, is a very simple one and one that
hopes others will see as requiring no justification.

> It is curiosity — the only kind of curiosity, at least, that is
> worth practising with some tenacity: not the curiosity that
> seeks to assimilate what one finds convenient to know, but
> the curiosity that allows one to get free of oneself. What is the
> point of all the labour involveed in research if the result is
> simply the acquisition of knowledge and not, as far as possi-
> ble, the bewilderment of him who knows? There are times in
> one's life when the question as to whether one can think
> otherwise than one does is indispensable if one is to go on
> looking and reflecting. (*Histoire de la Sexualité, II, L'Usage
> des Plaisirs*)

What is philosophy today, Foucault asks, if not the critical
work on thought itself? But early in his career, in the wake of
Heidegger and Husserl, Sartre and Merleau-Ponty, Foucault
had decided that he would not succeed in achieving that
égarement, that bewilderment, that losing of one's way without knowing it and finding oneself in some unexpected place,
by working within philosophy itself. Guided by the light of

Nietzsche's sun, as he put it, he traced the genealogy of reason and was led to the madhouse. After *Madness and Civilization,* it is difficult to have trust in either the practices or the pronouncements of psychiatrists. After *The Order of Things,* discourses lose their continuities and boundaries, their self-evident relation to things. After *Discipline and Punish,* we can no longer look at our twentieth-century societies through nineteenth-century eyes. Finally, at the end of his career, he looked at what we call our sexuality and decided, after jettisoning whole volumes of work, to examine the views of those writing at the very beginning of our European culture. What did he find? That all men were practising bisexuals, with one wife but many male sexual partners. That discussion of their homosexual relations belonged to a subject called erotics, while their heterosexual relations were discussed under the headings of civics and home economics — and women's own sexuality was not discussed at all. After returning from such alien territory, it is difficult to regard our own everyday sexual theories and practices as universal, permanent or normal, or to give credence to such arcane notions as the Name-of-the-Father or the assumption of one's Oedipus.

Foucault chose the word *égarement* to describe what he hoped to get out of his work and therefore, by implication, what we might get out of it. The choice of word is masterly and I suspect that Foucault knew it. But he could not have known how rich a seam he was laying down there: like all good writers he said more than he knew. Only a translator, faced with the impossible task of translating it could begin to appreciate this. My first attempt was 'bewilderment': not a bad choice, the suggestion of 'wild' is there, but quite inadequate. I went on to produce a gloss: *égarement* was rather 'losing one's way without knowing it and finding oneself in some unexpected place'. More simply, *s'égarer* can mean 'to be lost', but it can also mean 'to be in error', to wander, mentally as well as physically, 'to be crazy'. ·

Can Foucault really mean to suggest this: that he seeks to be in error (that is, not in Truth), to verge on madness? Yes, I think he does, in the sense that Truth is seen as safe, comfortable, familiar, home. The author of *Madness and Civilization,* with his team of literary madmen — Hölderlin, Nerval, Nietzsche, Roussel, Artaud — was well aware how close to madness those who wander far away from Truth can get. *Egarer* is, in a sense, a negation of *garer*, to garner, to store the harvest, to garage the car. Foucault is not for those who put away their thoughts as one puts away a car, always in the same place. He does not offer comfortable words; his books provide no shelter.

He never gave epigraphs to any of his books until the last, when a quotation from his friend, the poet René Char, appeared on the back of these latest two volumes in the *History of Sexuality*. Though the words of another, they are in a sense his last words: '*L'histoire des hommes est la longue succession des synonymes d'un même vocable. Y contredire est un devoir.*' They might be translated thus: 'The history of mankind is the long succession of synonyms of the same word. It is our duty to oppose them'. Foucault had a horror of repetition, hated synonyms. We shall never know where his opposition to the Same would have taken him next. What we have lost are several more trips into the unknown.

USES AND ABUSES OF MICHEL FOUCAULT
Jeffrey Weeks

I write as a historian whose work has been very much influenced by a reading of Michel Foucault. But I speak also as someone whose preoccupations, whilst superficially similar in many ways to those of the later Foucault, in fact pre-date any serious encounter with his work. For something like twelve years I have been researching and writing about the history and sociology of sexuality, and have been particularly preoccupied with three key aspects. In the first place, I have tried to explore the complexities of sexual identities, and in particular the historical emergence of a modern homosexual identity. In my book *Coming Out* and in various articles I have tried to show how the contemporary lesbian and gay identities are products not of nature or the the imperatives of desire but of social categorisation and self-definition, in a complex, shifting history. Secondly, and obviously closely related to this, I have tried to understand the relationship between the social and the sexual, and the changing focus of the social regulation of sexuality — an endeavour which culminated in my last book, *Sex, Politics and Society*. Thirdly, I have for a long time been interested in the dubious origins of sexology, the would-be science of sex — and of the truth of our nature. Almost the first thing I wrote on sex was an essay on Havelock Ellis, and in my most recent book I have tried to show how little Nature has to do with our contemporary sexual beliefs — and behaviours[1].

The point I want to emphasise is that all these preoccupations, and two of the three books, were conceived and largely written before I had read Foucault. I say this not to claim any special prescience, but to underline why I, like many other radical historians and sociologists, have been drawn to his work: not because of any fashionable chasing after the latest Parisian mode, nor because of any weakening of progressive commitment; but because his corpus of work seemed highly relevant to what appeared as intractable theoretical and political problems in work that was already creatively going on.

Foucault's writings offer no alternative theory or politics, though inevitably they have theoretical and political implications. Their impulse is analytical and critical, deconstructionist rather than positive. Like his friend Gilles Deleuze, he insists on treating theory as a 'box of tools' to be taken up and used as we need them. We are not under any obligation to accept all his positions. There is, indeed, much that is ambiguous in his work; some of his history can be, and should be, disputed as history; his political friends have sometimes been dubious, and his political positions muted. His work can and should be contested. But as he said of Nietzsche's work,

> I prefer to utilise the writers I like. The only valid tribute to thought such as Nietzsche's is precisely to use it, to deform it, to make it groan and protest.[2]

In the same way we must use Foucault — not to arm ourselves with a new orthodoxy but to ask old questions in new ways, and new questions of old problems.

In the rest of this paper I want to pick out three areas where it seems to me his influence has been wholly beneficial in contributing to reassessments of critical issues: in thinking through the relationship between history and politics; in developing a critique of sexual essentialism; and in the analysis of new social antagonisms and political subjectivities.

History and politics

It has become a commonplace on the Left that many of the most important contributions to radical political analysis in recent years have been in the form of historical investigation. But there is no easy or straightforward way of marrying 'history' and 'politics'[3]. Two approaches have been particularly common. The first is 'history as a lesson'. Here the stress is on learning from the past in order to understand the present and find guidelines for the future. History has a heuristic function which sensitizes us to the complexities of our contemporary world. If history repeats itself, we are given to understand, it is less likely to repeat itself as farce if we already know of the tragedy. Unfortunately, this assumes a transparent past whose warnings are clear, and alas, history never moves along a single tramline: its discontinuities are as evident as its continuities. More crucially, how do we really know that we know the past? If the past is a foreign country its languages can baffle the most agile translator. 'The horrid spectacle is seen,' Nietzsche wrote, 'of the mad collector raking over all the dust heaps of the past'[4] — and still coming up with the wrong answer. A second characteristic approach offers us 'history as exhortation'. The chief note here is the advice to the class, or nation, or gender, or oppressed minority to listen to its past, to find in its buried glories the moral example and histories of resistance to give us strength in present difficulties, to rescue, as E.P. Thomson powerfully put it, the downtrodden from the 'enormous condescension' of posterity, and of historians. At its best this strategy can evoke lost worlds of struggle, investigate hidden byways, reassess the way we see the development to the present. It recovers from the victors the pain, work and aspirations of the vanquished. It challenges us to challenge their defeat and looks to their triumph. But at its worst it can provide only a consoling myth, a false hope, an unrealistic reading of the present based on a false image of the past and an unrealisable hope for the future. In such an approach there is a real danger that the dead might well end up burying the living.[5]

A third approach seems to me more appropriate today for the investigation of our current discontents: to see history and politics as inextricably combined, to attempt to understand the ways in which the past has a hold on, organises and defines the contemporary perception. The aim is to understand 'the present' as a particular constellation of historical forces, to find out how our current political dilemmas have arisen, to see, in a word, the present as historical. What is needed is a history of the historical present as a site of definition, regulation and resistance. Hisory and politics in this reading are not uneasy bedfellows: they are essential partners.

Hence the appeal of Foucault's advocacy of a 'history of the present'. He is not so much concerned with analysis of the past as with the uncovering of what he describes as traces of the present. There is a rich diversity in his writings: from his early studies of psychology and madness, through the birth of modern medicine and the sciences of man, to the analysis of modern disciplinary forms and the four volumes

of the *History of Sexuality*. Beneath this variety there have
been two, closely related concerns: to expose the conditions
for the emergence of modern forms of rationality, especially
as expressed in the 'human sciences'; and to construct 'a
history of the different modes by which, in our culture,
human beings are made subjects'.

Clearly this is a specific sort of history — what Cousins
and Hussain call 'case history'[6] concerned not with an exhaustive searching out of the truth of the past but with the
intelligibility of the present. He has located an area of interest
which has hitherto been little investigated, the history of the
discursive realm, and has set out to investigate a precise
intellectual problem: the nature of the relationship between
the discursive and the non-discursive as it structures those
grids of meaning which organise the present. He does not
deny the validity of other types of history, but his concern is
elswhere: in understanding the mechanisms of thought and
action which delimit our modernity.

The scandal (for some), and the attraction for others is that
he does this without recourse to any master scheme of history or ultimate theory of causation. In Foucault the task of
historical investigation is not to seek a real history that slides
inexorably under the surface of events or works invisibly
behind humanity's back, but to address itself to these surfaces, the grids of meaning and language, which *are* 'the real'
in the way we live social relations. He compares what he calls
a general history with total history[7]. Total history attempts
to draw all phenomena round a single causative centre or
spirit of a society or civilisation. The same form of historical
influence is then seen to be operating on all levels, the economic, the social, the political, the religious, with the same type
of transformation and influences playing on all these levels.
General history, on the other hand, is concerned with 'series,
segmentations, limits, differences of level, time lags,
anachronistic survivals, possible types of relation'. The aim is
not however to offer a jumble of different histories, nor the
investigation of analogies or coincidences between them.
Nor is it a simple revival of crude positivism, of 'one damn
thing after another'. The task proposed by general history is
precisely to determine what forms of relation may legitimately be made between the various constituents of 'the
present'. This present is not a homogeneous product of a

unified history. It is more a promiscuous amalgam of specific histories, whose relationship it is the task of analysis to uncover. So what he calls — after Nietzsche — his genealogical method, is not concerned with the origin of the present, but with beginnings; not with causes but with emergences and effects.

The ultimate aim of all this, as Foucault puts it, is a diagnosis of the present, for history is a 'curative science'. And 'the purpose of history, guided by genealogy, is not to discover the roots of our identity but to commit ourselves to its dissipation'[8], to refuse those categorisations that are imposed upon us as truth. Clearly an approach such as this radically challenges any general theory of history and of society. There is no transhistorical economy which provides the substratum for a social superstructure, no society whose laws silently shape the imperatives of daily life. The 'economic', like 'the social' and 'the sexual' are themselves discursive unities whose histories, and temporal coexistence, must be traced. With such a radical scepticism about the fixity of social phenomena and their relationship one to the other, no rational theory of the world seems possible. But if we look at the implications of Foucault's work from another angle, then something more constructive appears. He does not deny that complex relationships between, say, the economic, the social, the familial, the sexual exist. He challenges us to investigate them in their singular emergence. We are encouraged to move away from an unthinking reliance on abstract determinism and a deterministic functionalism and urged to probe the actual relationship between one social form and another, the actual mechanics of power. The explanations are not written before the investigation nor deduced from first principles, and this must surely be a healthy emphasis in our efforts to understand the historic present.

It is a partial, limited but critical approach. It urges us to address ourselves to different analyses of events. It offers no magic solutions, but it directs us to find sharper perspectives on the working of power.

The history of sexuality

At the heart of our present is the continent of sexuality and its claim to hold the key to the truth of our individuality.

Throughout the 1970s a large number of people, chiefly
products of modern feminism and gay politics, battled with
theoretical and political questions about sex: about the historical forces that shaped sexuality, about the relationship
between capitalism and the construction of sexual difference
and sex oppression, about the relevance of sexual liberation
to socialist politics. These were not new questions on the
Left. They have been consistently asked both in the libertarian and Marxist traditions of socialism since the mid-
nineteenth century. What is striking, however is the dearth
of useful responses to these problems from the traditional
Left. Perry Anderson recently confessed that there were
blind spots in the Marxist tradition — with regard to war and
peace, the meaning of nature, women's oppression and the
possibilities of a 'socialist morality'[9]. But in this elegant
restatement of classical Marxism there seems to be no room
for rethinking the meaning of sexuality. Certain questions
are never asked — perhaps because they cannot be asked
within the inherited framework of socialist thought. Its
priorities have been elsewhere: in class relations, the state,
political organisation. For those of us on the Left who were
interested in questions of sexual politics as well, there was no
useful echo in the Marxist tradition. It was at this point of
deadlock that Foucault's work appeared as relevant.

Foucault's *History of Sexuality* is not, of course, a history
of behaviours or beliefs or of the highways and byways of
desire[10]. True to his general approach it is a study of the
emergence, development and effects of a specific configuration of discourses and practices. This has become clearer still
with the publication of volumes two and three of the *History*
where the conditions for the emergence of the whole apparatus are slowly and majestically being delineated. Foucault
no more offers a total theory of sexuality than he does of
history or politics. But in asking certain key questions, in
challenging various received ideas, in analysing crucial con-
nections he has contributed to a rethinking of the whole
relationship between the social and the sexual.

A central feature of the work is a critique of sexual
essentialism — and this is in line with his wider project.
Madness, the ostensible subject of Foucault's first major
text[11], and sex, the apparent theme of his most recent, seem
eminently natural objects to study. There are commonsens-

ical definitions of their nature, and untold texts detailing their abundant manifestations. A history of these phenomena, therefore, it might be supposed, could only be a history of attitudes toward them. But it is Foucault's main task precisely to question the naturalness and inevitability of these historical objects. Their pre-existence as natural unchanging objects is not to be taken for granted. All his work is based on this assumption but it becomes increasingly explicit as his work develops. In *Madness and Civilisation* he does not, of course, claim that phenomena to which the term madness can refer never existed. On the contrary, in this work there is a strong romantic naturalism, which gives the impression that Foucault is posing the truth of madness against the falsity of reason. But even here the main concern is with the way reason was conceptually separated from unreason, to provide the conditions for the emergence of modern psychiatric medicine. It is the social categorisation which unifies the disparate phenomena known collectively as 'madness'. By the time he comes to write the first volume of *The History of Sexuality* the lingering naturalism has all but disappeared. In this book, sex, far from being the object to which sexual discourse refers, is a phenomenon constructed within the discourse itself. He does not deny the existence of the material body, with its desires, aptitudes, potentialities, physical functions and so on, but he argues that the historian's task is to reread the discursive practices which make them meaningful and which change radically from one period to another. Why is it, he asked in the mischievously iconoclastic first volume of the *History,* that the Christian West has been so obsessed with sex, has given it such a central symbolic significance, that we can claim to know ourselves by knowing our sex? Is it possible, he wondered, far from being repressed, sexuality has been encouraged and produced as a central element in the operation of power? Could it be that in the very belief that through our sexuality we can be free, we are most truly enslaved?

It has to be said that few of Foucault's speculations were original or new in themselves[12]. Post-Kinsey sex research had convincingly demonstrated that sexuality was socially constructed, and Foucault's work is saturated with its findings. Feminists had begun investigating what Foucault was to call 'technologies of power' around sexuality long before his work appeared, especially with regard to the regulation of prostitution. Gay historians had already demonstrated the historical peculiarity of a 'homosexual species' and identity. Freudo-Marxists such as Marcuse had already vividly painted the shape of that gilded cage that paraded under the name of the sexual revolution. What Foucault offered was something more than all these: a powerful image of a great domain of sexuality which had a history — beginnings in the Christian preoccupations with sin and salvation, a middle in various strategies of regulation and control, of women, of children, of procreative behaviour and of sexual perversity; and a possible point of resistance in the evocation of the 'body and its pleasures'.

It was also, of course, a partial picture. Foucault's emphasis on the imprisoning nature of the categories of thought which organise how and what we can think seemed to leave little room for resistance and change. The challenge to the fixity of sexual identity seemed to undermine the need for any coherent sense of identity at all. Could he really be advocating what he once described as 'the happy limbo of a non-identity' [13], with its implied abnegation of any organising ego? And if sexuality was simply a ruse of power, no rational choices about sexual relations seemed possible. Was Foucault really denying the need for sexual politics or simply subverting their more bloated pretentions?

Foucault has tackled many of these issues in interviews and lectures since 1976, and indirectly responds to his articles in the two new volumes of the History, *L'Usage des Plaisirs* and *Le Souci de Soi.* He has shifted from analysing how people are defined, categorised and subjected to the tyrannies of sex, to how people, in a culture antecedent to our own, were defining themselves as subjects of ethical choice around the erotic. In place of describing the modes of modern sexuality as once promised, he now seeks to throw the whole edifice into historical relief by looking at its predecessors. And in place of our current Western belief that in sex lies truth, we are shown how the erotic, whilst still an object of moral concern, can take its part not at the centre of existence but as one aspect of an aesthetics of existence. We are nudged quietly into thinking what such a concept could mean for us today.

I do not particularly want to endorse all of this. The whole work on sexuality as it has now emerged can be challenged in historic detail, and no doubt that will be done by professionals for years to come. But whatever our detailed criticisms, this is a very important body of work and it poses three major questions. The first is historical. What is the relationship between the apparatus of sexuality and the diverse workings of power? Why and by what processes has sexuality come to the heart of our contemporary discourses? What is the relationship between the regulation of sexuality and other relations of exploitation and oppression? Foucault's answers are necessarily tentative, indirect, oblique. But these are vital questions and are posed more clearly than ever before.

Secondly, the work as a whole asks testing theorectical questions, about the relationship between desire and social categorisation, between social regulation and subjectification, between definition and self-definition, power and resistance. I believe there is an important role here for the theory of the dynamic unconscious, a topic Foucault himself is notoriously sceptical about. But again, in failing to offer positive guidelines, Foucault challenges us to rethink what we mean by subjectivity and its historically changing forms.

Thirdly, important political questions flow from Foucault's deconstruction of sexuality. One response to Foucault's challenge has been to deny the existence of any general categories — of women, of homosexuals, and to suggest that, in Stephen Heath's phrase, sexuality does not really exist, and therefore, by implication we can more or less slough off its pretentions[14]. This seems to me to be misguided. 'Sexuality' may be an historical invention but we are ensnared in its circle of meaning. We cannot escape it by act of will. This does not mean that we must simply accept the hegemonic definitions of our true sex handed down to us by theologians and sexologists. It does mean we need to rethink the criteria by which we can choose our sexualities. Foucault's work moves in the direction of a celebration of sexual diversity and choice, and his later interviews interestingly illustrate the degree to which he was working through some of the challenges this poses. The distinction he suggests between freedom of sexual acts and freedom of relationships, the first to be questioned because it might lead to a toleration of rape and violence, the second to be embraced because it

points to a new right to construct different forms of relations, breaks away from the sterile arguments about which
forms of activity are natural or unnatural, normal or abnor-
mal, and asks instead searching questions about context and
meaning and alternative forms of friendship. Far from denying the possibility of sexual change, Foucault beckons us to
think about it in different ways: not as a point of transcend-
ence to power, not as a mythic moment of liberation, but as a
possibility for inflecting the dominant codes, undermining
the truth claims of the arbiters of desire, and making new
relationships. As he put it in a late interview,

> We have to understand that with our desires, through our
> desires, go new forms of relationships, new forms of love,
> new forms of creation. Sex is not a fatality; it's a possibility
> for creative life.'[15]

Politics

This leads us finally to the political implications of
Foucault's work. He distinguishes in his paper on 'The
Subject and Power' between three types of struggles[16]
against forms of domination, whether ethnic, social or religious; against forms of exploitation that separate individuals
from what they produce; and 'against that which ties the
individual to himself and submits him to others' — that is
struggles against subjection, forms of subjectivity and sub-
mission. The first was dominant in the Middle Ages, the
second in the 19th century, the third is increasingly important today. This does not mean that the first two have been
superceded.

> It is certain that the mechanisms of subjection cannot be
> studied outside their relation to the mechanisms of exploita-
> tion and domination. But they do not merely constitute the
> 'terminal' of more fundamental mechanisms. They entertain
> complex and circular relations with other forms.[17]

This is fully in accord with Foucault's general reluctance to
see the present as constructed upon a single contradiction,
whether between capital and labour as the Marxist tradition
would prefer or between men and women as some feminists

might argue. The present is a mobile ensemble of specific histories, and manifests a host of social antagonisms. As Mouffe puts it:

> The emergence of new political subjects — women, national, racial and sexual minorities, anti-nuclear and anti-institutional movements, etc, are the expression of antagonisms that cannot be reduced to the relations of productions.[18]

The failure of the orthodox socialist tradition to address all, or any, of these new antagonisms and subjectivities, in an appealing way, has opened the door to alternative modes of analysis, either in the form of alternative universalisms, as in feminist theories of patriarchy, or in the microscopic investigation of specific modalities of power and domination, which has been the specific contribution of Foucault.

Again, therefore, we see that Foucault's approach fits in with a tendency amongst many on the Left to try to rethink the nature of contemporary struggles and to accord full recognition to the diversity of conflicts that fracture contemporary society: for Foucault 'power is constructed and functions on the basis of particular powers, myriad issues, myriad effects of power'.[19] It is a complex domain that must be analysed and combatted in the mechanisms and social practices through which power is actually exercised. This implies a multiplicity of struggles around specific configurations of power. It is, on the other hand, radically abstentionist about the possibility of forging links between the diverse struggles.

Foucault is deeply sceptical about the effectivity of programmes. Programmes, in a sense always fail, and we have to live with their unintended consequences. The programme of reforming the prisons in the early 19th century produced greater surveillance — and created criminals. The sexological programme of replacing moralistic definitions by scientific ones led to new forms of control over sexual diversity, and the imposition of new forms of correct behaviour. The revolutionary programme can lead as easily to the Gulag as to human liberation. We find in Foucault, therefore, no programme for social advance, no strategy for a new society.

But why should we seek it? Why should we look in the writings of a single intellectual for guidelines that others should follow in the future? For Foucault, the role of the intellectual in modern society is not to offer prescriptive analysis but to lay bare the mechanisms of power.

> The intellectual no longer has to play the role of an adviser. The project, tactics and goals to be adopted are a matter for those who do the fighting. What the intellectual can do is to provide instruments of analysis and at present this is the historian's essential role ... In other words, a topological and geological survey of the battlefield — that is the intellectual's role.[20]

Political conclusions are left to us, who are involved in the disparate conflicts of social life.

Foucault's rejection of the role of radical guru does not mean that links cannot be drawn between different struggles, that we cannot understand hierarchies of power, that political strategies are unnecessary or impossible — simply that we should not seek them in the body of work that Foucault himself produced. That strikes me as a wholly admirable modesty.

At the same time there is a more positive message we can learn from Foucault and especially from his later work. 'Maybe the target nowadays,' he suggests, 'is not to discover what we are, but to refuse what we are.' Against the insidious impact of modern power structures which simultaneously totalize and individualize we need to imagine what we could be:

> We have to promote new forms of subjectivity through the refusal of the kind of individuality which has been imposed on us for several centuries.[21]

The new political subjects that have emerged over the past 15 years illustrate a similar refusal of imposed definition. The Left ignores their challenge at its peril.

Notes

1. Jeffrey Weeks, *Coming Out: Homosexual Politics in Britain from the 19th Century to the Present*, London 1977; *Sex, Poli-*

tics and Society. The Regulation of Sexuality since 1800, London 1981; Sheila Rowbotham and Jeffrey Weeks, Socialism and the New Life, London 1977; Sexuality and its Discontents. Meanings, Myths and Modern Sexualities, 1985.

2. Michel Foucault, Power/Knowledge, edited by Colin Gordon, Brighton 1980, pp 53-4.

3. I am here loosely following the schema in Bill Schwarz, '"The People" in history: The Communist Party Historians' Group, 1946-56', in Contemporary Cultural Studies, Making Histories, London 1983.

4. F. Nietzsche, The Use and Abuse of History, Indianapolis 1979, P. 20.

5. Ibid, p. 16.

6. Mark Cousins and Athar Hussain, Michel Foucault, London 1984.

7. Michel Foucault, The Archaeology of Knowledge, London 1972, p. 3 ff.

8. See D.F. Bouchard (ed) Language, Counter-Memory, Practice. Selected Essays and Interviews, New York 1971, p. 156, 162.

9. Perry Anderson, In the Tracks of Historical Materialism, London 1983.

10. Michel Foucault, The History of Sexuality volume 1, An Introduction, London, Allen Lane 1978 (first French publication 1976); volume 2, L'Usage des Plaisirs, volume 3, Le Souci de Soi, Paris 1984.

11. Michel Foucault, Madness and Civilisation, London 1965.

12. For a full discussion of the sexological debates see my Sexuality and its Discontents.

13. Michel Foucault (ed), Herculin Barbin. Being the Recently Discovered Memoirs of a Nineteenth Century French Hermaphrodite, New York 1980.

14. Stephen Heath, The Sexual Fix, London 1982; see also debates in the Journal M/F.

15. 'Michel Foucault, An Interview: Sex, Power and the Politics of Identity' by Bob Gallagher and Alexander Wilson, The Advocate no. 400, 1984, p. 29.

16. Michel Foucault, 'The Subject and Power', Afterword in Herbert L. Dreyfus and Paul Rabinow, Michel Foucault. Beyond Structuralism and Hermeneutics, Brighton 1982.

17. Ibid, p. 213.

18. Chantal Mouffe, 'Hegemony and the Integral State in Gramsci: Towards a New Concept of Politics' in George Bridges and Rosalind Brunt (eds), Silver Linings. Some Strategies for the Eighties, London 1981, p. 167

19. Foucault, Power/Knowledge, p. 188

20. Ibid, p. 42

21. Foucault, 'The Subject and Power', op cit, p. 216.

FOUCAULT AND PSYCHOANALYSIS
John Forrester

I have a number of books to which I turn when in need of intellectual refreshment — I suppose top of the list is Freud. But in recent years, not far behind were the works of Michel Foucault. As a result, my personal reaction to the news of his death was that the flow of good books, of good matter to feed on, was stopped. I was going to have to go hungry in future. But it was not just my feeding that I experienced as interrupted — just as speedy was the sense that Foucault's work had been interrupted, entirely unjustly and without reason. Not just the projected six volume *History of Sexuality,* which I had never expected to see completed in, say, the sense we might hope for Needham's *Science and Civilization in China* to be completed. I expected as much to come from Foucault as I had been given by him to date.

Yet my reactions to Foucault were not always of this grateful and admiring character. In 1970, when I had first opened and read a book of his, my reaction was of mystified irritation. There I was, a young historian of science, looking for a way of analysing the biological and human sciences in the spirit of my mentor, Thomas Kuhn, looking for a sharp-nosed sociology of the institutions of science and a vigilant attention to the structure of scientific concepts, to decide what was a paradigm and what was pre-paradigmatic. What use could I make of a book that analysed *Le Neveu de Rameau* and Descarte's *Meditations*, Pascal and Nietzsche, alongside the philosophical anatomy of mania and melancholia of the eighteenth century? I set it to one side, irritated, confused, all the while not being able to forget some of its most poignant images or its most brilliant passages: the Ship of Fools, the sense of oppressive order and silence descending over the asylum as Pinel struck off the chains of the insane. And, most significantly for me, the enigmatic final pages in which Foucault describes the most recent attempt to come to terms with Unreason, that of Freud — an attempt

that founders, he surmises, because of the inescapable alienation that is built into the doctor-patient relation upon which
the psychoanalytic situation is constructed.

Those images — they do remain with you, however dis-
dainful and dismissive one's overall attitude to Foucault.
Each of his books has a passage that serves as a kind of
shorthand in talking with others about them. The 'death of
man' passage from *The Order of Things* — 'like a face drawn
in sand at the edge of the sea'. And the virtuoso analysis of
Las Meninas that opens that book. The opening description
of Damiens's corporeal destruction and the Panopticon in
Discipline and Punish. Images that are not so much un-
forgettable as riveting — they draw the sensibility tight to
them, and will not let go. Certainly it takes a specifically
dogged, though common enough puritanism to distrust and
deprecate the power of Foucault's images. I will return to
them later — for now, it is worth pointing out how, once one
has read his books, these images, so like dream images, act as
a kind of mnemonic for his argument. Once read and understood, one returns to the images as if they represented a
coded, shorthand version of what one has learned, an image
that sums up the argument the way a mathematical equation
is thought to sum up, to 're-present' an argument. Hence
discussions and criticisms of Foucault's texts may well be
couched in terms of an analysis or attack on his images — the
debate over his interpretation of *Las Meninas* seems to stand
in for a more difficult and arduous judgement on his account
of the theory of representation in the eighteenth century.
And the empiricist historian's discomfort is often, like my
own initial reaction, because of the difficulty of locating
these images: 'A new object makes its appearance in the
imaginary landscape of the Renaissance; soon it will occupy
a privileged place — the Ship of Fools.' (*Histoire de la Folie*,
p. 18). Where are we to locate this image? It appears as new
both to us and to the Renaissance. It is located in an 'imaginary landscape'. Where, we might ask, is that?

When I turned once again, after a lapse of some years, to
Foucault, my mental landscape had been transformed by a
study of Freud and, with great resistance, of Lacan. And
now, it was an entirely different author I was reading —
those sentences of Foucault's on Freud and the doctor-
patient relationship, together with *The Birth of the Clinic*,

revealed an entirely new way of thinking about the history of medicine and science: the logic of the gaze, the architecture, ordering and cataloguing of diseases within the hospital, indicated how perception, material practices and knowledges were articulated together. When read, as I then did, alongside *The Order of Things,* it was clear that Foucault's metahistory, as I thought of it then, or genealogy, as he began to talk of it, was an unrivalled, unprecedented attempt at organising systems of knowledge in a historical account, which represented both systemic coherence and explanatory force, and depicted the profound transformation of such systems, transformations which might well turn around seemingly 'surface' events. Admittedly, I had had an experience which made Foucault especially appealing — attempting to grapple with the complexities of eighteenth century physiology. I had got substantially nowhere tracing out the chains of influence of one theory on another, one doctor on another. And nor, so it seemed from looking at the scholarly literature, had anyone else. Foucault's work on the eighteenth century gave a framework to the amorphous mass of eighteenth century material in the life sciences and medicine, a framework which could be argued over, and argued with, but was without precedent.

Yet my concerns were and are elsewhere — with psychoanalysis and its history. So, I asked myself, where does psychoanalysis fit in to the various narratives Foucault gave? Tantalising at the end of *Madness and Civilisation:* implicit in *The Birth of the Clinic,* where a rigorous account of the 'modern' forms of the doctor-patient relationship was given; and explicit in *The Order of Things,* as one of the two new sciences, the other being ethnology, that broke up the order of nineteenth century sciences *from within.* What was more, Foucault's chapters on philology in the nineteenth century gave me moral and material support in my own attempt to argue the kinship, the genealogical relation, between philology and psychoanalysis. But Foucault seemed to me to be a little bit too coy about the historical position which Freud can be accorded, and, more to the point, the significance to be accorded to the interpretive strategies of psychoanalysis. Yet there was no reason to think that this sense of dissatisfaction was anything more than a derivative of my own desire that Foucault, who was so magisterial and encyclopaedic in other areas, address the domain which I was trying to make my own.

When *La volonté de savoir* came out, some of my questions were answered: it seemed as if psychoanalysis was the grandest and purest of the apparatuses for the generation of knowledge-power; the modern confessional discipline par excellence, and generator of a discourse that proclaimed evangelically that the truth of the subject was to be found in his or her secret discourse on sexuality. Indeed, Foucault wrote in that book that his enterprise could be read as the archaeology of psychoanalysis. Yet there was something too neat about the project: if the book were the archaeology of psychoanalysis, why was there so little textual reference, so little explicit addressing of themes in psychoanalysis? To me, it seemed clear that many arguments were implicitly aimed at psychoanalysis (amongst other things). Yet sometimes the other things were so vaguely evoked, so tangential, while the unnamed object was so obviously pshychoanalytic that I felt that there was something odd, refracted and displaced about the book. My curiosity was aroused.

My next step in tracking down Foucault's relation to psychoanalysis was to go and ask him about it. Remarkably enough, that was no help at all. Our quite lengthy discussion, while confirming and adding a new dimension to my admiration for him, gave me no sense whatsoever of what I deduced was a complex relation, even a complex genealogy. So I turned scholar instead of journalist, and read with the secret glee of the scholar-detective an early work of Foucault's, one that I have never seen discussed. Perhaps it is Foucault's earliest publication: the Introduction to a French translation of Ludwig Binswanger's *Traum und·Existenz.* Here I came upon a sense not only of Foucault's relation to psychoanalysis, but also of the seeds of other, probably more important, themes in his work. Foucault's Introduction, published in 1954, included a lengthy discussion both of Freudian interpretation, obviously focused on the dream, and of the theory of the subject in psychoanalysis. Here are two themes which are immediately apparent in Foucault's later work — the criticism of a variety of metaphysics of interpretation (the most obvious text here is *The Archaeology of Knowledge,* but one should not forget the critique of the techniques of the confessional targeted in *The History of Sexuality*, Vol 1) and of the concept of the subject it generates.

According to Foucault, the dream as analysed by Freud gains access to the *meaning* of the unconscious — it is a semantic analysis. But it leaves out of account the morphology of the imaginary:

> There is a different morphology of imaginary space when what is at issue is free, light-filled space, or when the space at work is that of the prison of obscurity and of suffocation. The imaginary world has its own laws, its specific structures — the image is a bit more than the immediate fulfilment of meaning; it has its own density, and the laws of the world are not solely the decrees of a single will, were that one divine.

It is also clear that Foucault's reading of Freud was already influenced by Lacan, as every recent French writer on psychoanalysis has been; but this is the Lacan of 1954, the Lacan of a metaphysics of full speech, of the necessarily deceptive functions of the imaginary. Foucault resisted this metaphysics of speech. He opposed both Klein and Lacan, and opposed them to each other, with the independent logic of the image, resistant to the linguistic interpretation, the speech-ocentrism, if you will allow me to say that, of psychoanalysis. Hence Foucault's interpretation of Dora sees her cure as *effective*, because the dream in which she announces the termination of the treatment maps out her struggle to escape from the interpretive strategies of Freud and all the others with whom she is in everyday contact, both men and women. It announces her means of escape from the iron law of Freud's theory of identification, in which every image of herself and of the others is just a representation, and a representation of something else. For Foucault, Dora becomes heroically, stoically cured through acknowledging her solitary destiny, by walking out on Freud. If she were to *say* it, she would only be subjected (in all the senses of the term) to Freud's steamrollering interpretive strategies. Dora's truth cannot be found along the path of psychoanalysis because the communication of psychoanalysis will leave the expressive force of the image untouched and will attempt to dispel it, since psychoanalysis is wholly committed to an analysis of representation, rather than expression. What is more, her truth will *only* be found by the solitary escape from the prison of representation.

It is not, then, all that strange to find Foucault's last two books, volumes II and III of *L'Histoire de la Sexualité,* returning to the question: what are the paths by which the truth of the subject may be constituted apart from the regime of knowledge-power that psychoanalysis so clearly embodies. Foucault's interest in Dora is now, thirty years on, translated into an interest in the Greeks and Romans. Yet, as many reviewers have noticed, these books are decidedly unexpected coming from Foucault, almost at odds with what we have known up to now of his work. Firstly, the question of power, which seemed so important in his work in the mid- to late-70s is almost totally absent. It is replaced by a concern with ethics: how is a sexual ethics constituted? The claim that Foucault accepts is that such an ethics contains two elements: a code of prohibitions and a method of subjectivation — a method of producing a subject of moral truth and action. For the Greeks and the Romans, it is practices of self-mastery that have precedence over the code of prohibition, and the function of this self-mastery is in relation to social ideals, rather than sacred truths. It thus seems as if these books are directed to ethical ends in the present, rather than epistemological, historical or political ends.

Secondly, the most surprising feature of these books is their style. There are none of the beautiful passages, the 'gleaming words' that Alan Sheridan talks of in his book on Foucault. There are no striking images. At times it seemed to me as if Foucault, like many another before him, had fallen under the spell of the Greeks — and not the spell of the Cynics, or the Sophists, but of the Master himself, of Aristotle. It seemed as if Foucault had taken on Aristotle and had succumbed, with that peculiar pleasure that comes from the somnolent, oh-so-clear-mindedness of the Stagyrite.

But I also have another explanation to offer as to why these books are so humble and austere: it is the thesis that Foucault, as a historian of the present, was first and foremost a historian of the failures and intellectual crises of the present. The shift from philosophy to psychopathology of the young Foucault of the 1940s was a recognition of philosophy's failure to offer up its secrets. The text I've discussed on 'Dream and Existence', and later *Madness and Civilisation,* were constructed on the failure of psychopathology and philosophy to encompass madness. The failures of Marxism and structuralism are mapped out in *The Order of Things*. And the failure of *gauchiste*, revolutionary politics is what gives *Discipline and Punish* its bite, with its dizzying,but secretly satisfying, masochistic analysis of the ubiquity of power. *La Volonté de Savoir* is the analysis of the failure of the movements of sexual liberation.

So, what is the failure being addressed in these last two books? I think it is the failure of the intellectual himself — Foucault's own failure. His refusal to be a guru did not prevent him from according a critical function to the intellectual — witness the myriad interviews which are avidly recorded and transcribed, commented upon and treasured for what is hoped to be found in them: a treasure-store of guides to action and legitimizing argument. With these last two books, the only trace left of the historian of the present is to be found in the initial question: how are the paths to becoming a subject of a practice to be mapped? And the domain here is no longer political or strategic. This is a moral quest, the *ascesis* Foucault talks of at the beginning of Volume II — an exercise of self-restraint, in which the style of the intellectual and the images of a freedom which is beyond the reach of interpretive recuperation were given up, without reluctance or nostalgia, in returning to Aristotle and Phidias.

FOUCAULT AND THE FRANKFURT SCHOOL
Peter Dews

In the final years of his life, probably as a result of increasing contact with scholars in the United States, Michel Foucault came to acknowledge clearly for the first time the affinities between his work and the concerns of the tradition of Critical Theory, and to consider his own thought as a contribution to a broader current of reflection on modern society. In a lecture on Kant's celebrated essay, 'What is Enlightenment?', given at the *Collège de France* shortly before he died, Foucault explicitly placed his own work in the line of thought concerned with what he terms — perhaps somewhat awkwardly — the 'ontology of actuality', and which he portrays as running from Kant and Hegel to the Frankfurt School, via Nietzsche and Weber.[1] Furthermore, in an interview with Gerard Raulet, Foucault admitted that he could have avoided many oversights and detours in his own work, had he been familiar with the Frankfurt School at an earlier date. 'It is a strange case,' he states, 'of non-penetration between two very similar types of thinking whch is explained, perhaps, by that very similarity.'[2]

On the other side, Jürgen Habermas has paid an unreserved obituary tribute to Foucault, suggesting that, from the circle of philosophical diagnosticians of contemporary society of his generation, Foucault has 'affected the spirit of the times most enduringly.'[3] Habermas prizes Foucault's work, above all, for its demonstration that 'the legal-administrative means for putting welfare state programmes into action do not represent a passive medium without properties of its own. Rather a practice of the isolation of facts, of normalization and surveillance is linked with them...'[4] This appreciation is simply one token of the fact that not only Foucault's work, but post-structuralist thought as a whole, is beginning to be stripped of its exclusivist claims and incorporated into a broader international debate on the nature of modernity.

The more particular convergences between Foucault and the Frankfurt School become vividly apparent if one compares the central contentions of *Discipline and Punish* with the arguments of Adorno and Horkheimer's *Dialectic of Enlightenment*, published over thirty years earlier, in 1944. In the assemblage of 'Notes and Drafts' which makes up the final section of their book, Adorno and Horkheimer introduce some reflections on the significance of the modern prison system which now read like a startling anticipation of Foucault. The prison is portrayed as exemplifying the plight of modern subjectivity, self-enclosed and severed from any lateral contact:

> The rows of cells in a modern prison are monads in the true sense of the word defined by Leibniz.... The monads have no direct influence on each other: their life is regulated and co-ordinated by God, or direction. Absolute solitude, the violent turning inward of the self, whose whole being consists in the mastery of material and in the monotonous rhythm of work, is the specter which outlines the existence of man in the modern world.

Furthermore, as in Foucault, the internalization of discipline by forcibly isolated subjects is seen as entailing a martyrization of the body. The minute regulation of the corporeal which, for Foucault, is the essence of disciplinary power corresponds to the elimination of sensuous spontaneity lamented by Horkheimer and Adorno, an alienation from our existence as *natural* beings. For the Critical Theorists, as for Foucault, and here their common Nietzschean inheritance is at its clearest, 'Europe has two histories: a well-known written history and an underground history. The latter consists in the fate of the human instincts and passions which are distorted and displaced by civilization.'[6]

Accordingly, both the work of Foucault and of the Frankfurt School is haunted by the idea of a 'utopia' of non-regulated seriousness. In *The History of Sexuality*, for example, Foucault permits himself to evoke fleetingly a 'different economy of bodies and pleasures' which would no longer be subordinate to the confessional quest for identity,[7] while in his *Negative Dialectics* Adorno argues that 'all happiness aims at sensual fulfilment and obtains its objectivity in that fulfilment. A happiness blocked off from every such aspect is no happiness.'[8]

Despite these thematic affinities, however, there is clearly a significant gap in the way in which reuglating power and its dominated other, and the relation between them, are theorized in the two cases. For the Frankfurt School the oppressiveness of this relation is the result of the preponderance in modern society of a restricted, means-end rationality, which cannot be seen as exhausting the promise of reason as such. This means that the corporeal is not seen as 'intrinsically' irrational: Freud's error, for example, is to take the conformist ego's view of the drives as threatening and chaotic for an immutable truth. Conversely, instrumental reason itself appears irrational from the standpoint of a suffering nature which it overrides. Each aspect of divided reason experiences the irrationality of its other. Foucault, of course, rejects this perspective, since — along with other post-structuralist thinkers — he suspects that the promise of an undivided reason has totalitarian implications. He is much more inclined to adopt Nietzsche's conception of an irreducible conflict between the Apollonian and the Dionysian. Correspondingly, Foucault rejects the notion of a single historical division of reason. He argues that we cannot speak of reason and its history as such, but only of a plurality of practices, of 'regimes of rationality', which compete and overlap with each other. Our task is to situate ourselves within this ever-shifting field of struggles, without anticipating any ultimate 'reconciliation'.

Power and Knowledge

Although Foucault's position does have a useful sobering effect, in its opposition to both optimistic and apocalyptic philosophies of history, it leaves him with some serious theoretical difficulties. Firstly, there is the question of the general connection between power and knowledge upon which his work of the 1970s, in particular, is based. Foucault's conceptualization of this connection is remarkably labile and elusive. Although his evident intention is to present power and knowledge as internally related (hence his use of the hyphenated term, 'power-knowledge)', this relation is in fact most frequently portrayed in terms of the *institutional preconditions* for the formation of certain types of knowledge: Foucault's fundamental argument is that it is the opportunities for close surveillance opened up by the asylum, the hospital, the prison, which make possible the elaboration of the corresponding 'human sciences'. Thus, in an interview dating from 1975 he suggests that:

> The archaeology of the human sciences has to be established through studying the mechanisms of power which have invested human bodies, acts and forms of behaviour. And this investigation enables us to rediscover one of the conditions of the emergence of the human sciences: the great 19th century effort in discipline and normalization. [9]

But to talk in this way is in fact to make the relation between power and knowledge non-intrinsic: Foucault does not explain how the 'effort in discipline and normalization' is *enhanced* by the application of scientific knowledge. The reason for this failure is not difficult to discover. For, were Foucault to admit that the application of scientific knowledge increases the effectivity of action, he would be obliged to abandon his underlying relativist stance, and to admit the reality of 'progress' in at least one dimension of rationality, the cognitive-instrumental dimension. Hence the crossing of the 'technological' threshold by disciplines, the spiralling reinforcement of power and knowledge which Foucault evokes,[10] remains theoretically unexplained.

Secondly, there is a deep difficulty in Foucault's accounts of the relation between disciplinary power and the body, reason and its 'other'. Since Foucault wishes to avoid judging power-knowledge complexes from an epistemological standpoint, believing that no such standpoint can be philosophically sustained, and therefore refuses to draw a distinction between facticity and validity, he cannot denounce the oppressive human sciences as forms of distortion or misrepresentation. For Foucault, as we know most clearly from *The Archaeology of Knowledge*, the 'objects' of discursive formations are defined *by* these formations. But this abstention from judgements of validity leads to difficulties when Foucault wishes to give his position a critical edge. An attack of discplinary power, for example, could only be carried out from the standpoint of an alternative conception of the body:

but for Foucault this second conception could only be part of another power-knowledge complex, and could not claim any greater 'truth' or normative superiority. Foucault's response to this dilemma remains fundamentally ambiguous. On the one hand he is tempted to abandon his critical claims, suggesting that

> It is necessary to pass over to the other side - the other side from the "good side" - in order to try to free oneself from these mechanisms which made two sides appear, in order to dissolve the false unity of this other side whose part one has taken. [11]

On the other hand. Foucault is clearly unable entirely to abandon a liberatory perspective. But this perspective is condemned to remain tentative and fleeting, since it seems to require, in contrast to the Frankfurt Schools's attack on the irrationailty of the dominant *ratio*, an espousal of irrationality itself.

These difficulties in Foucault's approach make it legitimate to enquire whether Foucault's relativistic dispersion of rationalities is the appropriate reaction to the project of restoring a bisected reason, and indeed whether this project has the totalitarian implications which Foucault assumes. It is arguable, for example, that Adorno sees self-contradiction precisely in reason's claim to totality, and envisages a utopia in which thought and its other would enter into a non-reductive equilibrium.[12] But, even setting this question aside, a case can be made that Foucault is misled by a conflation which brings him remarkably close to, rather than opposing him to, the first generation of the Frankfurt School. Throughout his work Foucault suggests that the emergence of the universal dimension of bourgeois subjectivity leads to a totalization of social control. This suggestion emerges particularly clearly in an interview on Bentham's Panopticon which Foucault gave in the mid-'70s. Here Foucault affirms that:

> Bentham was the complement of Rousseau. What was in fact the dream that motivated many of the revolutionaries? It was the dream of a transparent society, visible and legible in each of its parts, the dream of there no longer existing any zones of

darkness, zones established by the privileges of royal power
or the prerogatives of some corporation, zones of disorder....
Thus Bentham's obsession, the technical idea of the exercise
of an all-seeing power, is grafted on to the great Rousseauist
theme which is in some sense the lyrical note of the
Revolution. [13]

The Politics of Enlightenment

This equation of the politics of Enlightenment with an increasing manipulation of society can also be found in the
thought of Horkheimer and Adorno. Yet, in contrast to
Foucault, the Critical Theorists are unable entirely to over-
look the progressive aspect of bourgeois conceptions of legal
and political rights. In the foregoing quotation Foucault
appears to equate surreptitiously the resistance of popular
disorder with the opacity of the arcane politics of feudal and
absolutist monarchies, whereas Horkheimer and Adorno
never forget that feudal institutions are not simply impe-
dances to the all-seeing gaze of the state, but also enshrine
cruel and unjustifiable inequalities between human beings.
Adorno points out that the 'internalization of society as a
whole', which Foucault can only portray in terms of subjection to the disciplinary mechanism, 'replaces the reflexes of a
feudal order whose structure splinters what is universal in
mankind.' In the same passage he reminds us that 'once the
rational unity of the will is established as the sole moral
authority, the subject is protected from the violence done to
it by a hierarchical society.'[14]

In the work of Jürgen Habermas, this progressive dimension of Enlightenment universality is given more comprehensive treatment. Adorno can only conceive of this universality as indifferent to individuals, and individual impulse,
and therefore remains profoundly ambivalent towards it.
Whereas Habermas sees general accord not as something
imposed on individuals but as something to be achieved
through discussion. Habermas's account of the development
of a bourgeois 'public sphere' in the course of the eighteenth
century, of the emergence of the notion that the exercise of
political power should be subjected to the judgement of
public opinion, makes clear how mistaken Foucault is to see

in the reign of opinion only the tyrannous gaze of the Panopticon.[15] Probably because, in considering the theoretical foundations of bourgeois democracy, he has Rousseau's idea of a prediscursive unanimity of feeling in mind, Foucault overlooks the fact that the freedom and equality of genuine discussion are necessarily opposed to the hierarchies of power. In *Discipline and Punish* Foucault does emphasize, and implicitly criticize, the fact that disciplinary power cuts off lateral communication between subjects,[16] but he has no means of giving this fact any theoretical or political weight, since — like other post-structuralist thinkers — he pays insufficient attention to the intersubjective dimension of language, tending to theorize discourse in terms of hierarchies of monological power, 'regimes of truth'. Consequently, the demands of the body can also only appear for Foucault in the prediscursive, and therefore irrational, forms of what he terms 'resistance': they cannot be introduced into the fluidity of a discussion which is concerned with the consensual establishment of norms. There appears to be, throughout the majority of Foucault's work, an irresoluble contradiction between corporeal spontaneity and the formation and development of self-consciousness.

It was doubtless in part because of his awareness of this *impasse* that Foucault, in his last books, abandoned the original plan of his proposed 'history of sexuality', and returned to explore the ethical codes of Greek and Roman antiquity. In *L'Usage des Plaisirs* and *Le Souci de Soi* Foucault seeks to portray a form of self-control which is authentic self-determination, rather than subjection to a universal law. Moderation and restraint are no longer internalized power, but the personal striving towards an 'aesthetics of existence'. But despite the severe beauty of Foucault's evocations, the notion of a self-imposed stylisation of life which he outlines in these works, dependent — as it is — upon evident disparities of privilege and power, not least between the sexes, must surely be considered as a final disillusioned retreat from the problems of the present, rather than as a contribution to their resolution. For no serious consideration of the dilemmas of modernity can ultimately afford to retreat from the ideals of democracy and equality which are so central to modern consciousness. It is in the appreciation of this fact, and of the additional complexities which it brings, that the decisive difference between Foucault and the Frankfurt School lies.

Notes

1. See Michel Foucault, 'Un Cours Inédit', in *Magazine Littéraire*, 207, May 1984, pp.35-39.
2. 'Structuralism and Post-Structuralism: An Interview with Michel Foucault', *Telos* 55, Spring 1983, p. 00.
3. See Jürgen Habermas, 'Genealogische Geschichtschreibung', *Merkur* 429, October 1984, p. 784.
4 . Jürgen Habermas, 'Die Neue Unübersichtlichkeit', *Merkur* 431 January 1985, p.7.
5. Theodor Adorno and Max Horkheimer, *Dialectic of Enlightenment*, London 1979, p. 226.
6. *Dialectic of Enlightenment*, p. 231.
7. Michel Foucault, *The History of Sexuality*, Harmondsworth 1981, p. 159
8. Theodor Adorno, *Negative Dialectics*, London 1973, p. 202.
9. Michel Foucault, 'Body/Power' in *Power/Knowledge*, Brighton 1980, p. 61.
10. Michel Foucault, *Discipline and Punish*, Harmondsworth 1977, p. 225
11. Michel Foucault, 'Non au Sexe Roi', *Le Nouvel Observateur*, 644, 12-21 March 1977, p. 113.
12. This is the basis of the critique of Hegel which runs through Adorno's Negative Dialectics.
13. Michel Foucault, 'The Eye of Power', in *Power/Knowledge*, p.152
14. *Negative Dialectics*, p. 239.
15. See Jürgen Habermas, *Strukturwandel der Offentlichkeit*, Neuwied 1962.
16. In *Discipline and Punish* Foucault affirms of the prisoner that 'He is seen, but he does not see; he is the object of information, never a subject in communication.' (p. 200).

THE RISE AND FALL OF FRENCH MARXISM
Gareth Stedman Jones

What we're here to discuss is the rise and fall of French Marxism, particularly French structural Marxism over the last twenty or thirty years. What I want to do to begin with is give a very simple introduction, trying to set the French Marxism of these years in some sort of historical context, and to talk in particular about the role of Althusser since he represents the most serious attempt at re-theorization of a Marxist, or more precisely of a Marxist-Leninist perspective, in the 1960s and early 70s. The failure of that political-theoretical project has had very important consequences for the fate of Marxism, not just in France, but in all other advanced countries as well.

The first brief point I want to make is that Althusser originally made his name outside France for his novel reading of what Marxist theory actually meant. But although this was indeed a brilliant theorization in its own terms, it wasn't by any stretch of the imagination an accurate theorization of what historically Marx actually intended, or what his theory was about.

One of the most distinctive things, I think, about the Althusserian theorization of Marx, particularly if one takes it from *For Marx* and *Reading Capital*, is the way in which what, for Marx, had been a central dialectic between the forces and relations of production, virtually disappears from the analysis; and the forces of production – the actual level of material progress achieved by a particular society – are simply transposed into being a subset of the relations of production. What this actually means is that the way in which Althusser wants to reread Marxism, and in particular Marx's theory of the capitalist mode of production, is in a sense as an eternity. That is to say that it is a contradictory relationship, yes, but it is one that endlessly reproduces itself. And the forces that might bring down capitalism are not so much actually produced by history – or at least not produced by any inherent tendency within the capitalist mode of production – but rather come as a moment of dissolution, provoked almost from outside in what Althusser originally called 'the unity in rupture'.

So I think the first point to register is that whatever Althusser was talking about, he wasn't talking, nor was he I think seriously intending to talk, in very accurate historical terms about trying to retrieve the original theory of Marx.

It is important to remember that Marx thought he had constructed a theory not only of the reproduction of the capitalist mode of production, but also of a tendency towards self-destruction and self-transcendence inherent within this mode of production and manifested through the advance of the forces of production, represented by the rising organic composition of capital. That meant more factories and a larger industrial proletariat, in crude terms, which was going to create a polarization of society, resulting in a series of worsening crises and eventually leading to a stage beyond capitalism, and finally to a classless society.

Now if Althusser didn't represent an adequate theorization of Marx, what on the other hand he did represent was a very accurate and loyal theorization of the political practice and political writings of Lenin. If one does not understand that the emotional centre of Althusser is a defence of Leninism in all its aspects – the Leninist Party, and of course, the achievement of the Russian Revolution through the Bolshevik Party – then one has understood little about Althusser. Indeed, a lot of his actual reconceptualization of what Marxism was, can only be understood in these terms.

What Althusser represents – if we pose it not simply as a theory *sub spece eternitatis*, but as an actual theory produced by a member of the French Communist Party in the course of the 1960s – is an attempt to defend the legitimacy and the authority of the French Communist Party in a situation which is obviously very different from that which produced 1917 in Russia.

For instance, some of you may be familiar with Althusser's position on humanism. In the period after 1956 in which the French Communist Party tried to move away from overt identification with Stalinist practice and attempted to express this by espousing a notion of humanism, Althusser's intervention, in particular his attack on humanism, must be

seen as an attempt to reinforce the authority of the traditional
Leninist Party before 1956. The way he does so is as follows.
The general argument had been, both within the Party itself
and among fellow travellers accompanying the Party, that
the way to understand Marx at his most generous was to look
at the texts of the early Marx which talk about the alienation
of the human condition – a general condition suffered by
more or less everybody in capitalist society or a society based
on property. The problem of this approach for Althusser was
that if you actually follow that road, then what particular
reason is there for prioritizing the role of a proletarian party.
If everyone is alienated, why is it particularly the proletarians
who are the unique source of emancipation?

Althusser — and this is both a statement of his conservatism and his intellectual novelty — cut the Gordian knot here
by saying that the situation of alienation and what produced
the situation of mystification, that is, the inability to perceive
reality and the fact that reality could only be apprehended
through scientific effort, was a permanent state of the human
condition. This was not a situation which could be relieved
by a proletarian revolution. Alienation was, of course, pre-
eminent in the thought of the *young Marx*. But there was also
an *old Marx*, and Althusser makes a great point of dividing
one from the other. The *old Marx*, the Marx who, in Althusser's words, discovered the science of history, is also the
Marx who dropped the notion of alientation and who com-
pletely redefined the notion of fetishism of commodities in
such a way that the notion of alienation is no longer relevant.
What matters about the mature Marx, according to Althusser, is his conception of surplus value as it is presented in
Capital, and it is that which must be overcome in order to
transcend capitalism.

This is quite neat in the sense that it both introduces a
strong distinction between Marx before 1845 and afterwards
and implies the thought that somehow alienation is the sort
of conception with which petty bourgeois well-wishers of
socialism may adorn the theory of Marxism, but it does not
belong to the corpus of Marx's *scientific* works. It also has the
great advantage of preserving the Party as the guardian of
Marx's scientific discovery, that of surplus value.

The third point I would like to lead onto from this is that,
of course, if your deepest political instincts are to try to

preserve the vistas of Leninism and the role of a Leninist Party in a situation which by the 1960s in France is far from that of the Czarist state before 1917, then there is a difficulty in actually distinguishing between Leninism and Stalinism. This is a problem which Althusser tries to address several times in a very tortured way.

Everyone, of course, says they are against Stalinism. But if asked to define more specifically what Stalinism actually is, the question is by no means an easy one to answer, particularly if one is a Leninist. What one finds in Althusser is constant reference to 'tragedies' and 'terrible events', but we are never told what these 'tragedies' and 'terrible events' are. In other words, the crimes of Stalinism, however they are conceived, are never named. In a way, it is difficult for Althusser to mention them, simply because if one believed in collectivization or believes that socialism after the revolution will continue the class struggle though by other means — as Althusser did — then it is difficult to argue or to know exactly what it is about Stalinism which constitutes a deviation from Leninist practice. Since the Leninist Party is sacrosanct, Stalinism cannot be attributed to the excesses of a certain form of political organization or political authority. Leninism, of course, also rules out any idea of pluralism in matters of Marxist-Leninist theory.

From a strict Marxist-Leninist position, I think Althusser is also correct to criticize the Soviet Union for arguing that all that was wrong with Stalinism was the cult of personality. The cult of personality is not a very Marxist explanation for the Stalinist excesses of the Soviet Union in the 1930s and 40s. He is also correct in my opinion to suggest the inadequacy of the Trotskyite notion of Stalinism as simply a phenomenon deriving from Stalin himself and his closest henchmen. Such an explanation is evasive and superficial since it refuses any connection between Stalinism and Bolshevism.

But having said all that, Althusser is then faced with his own explanation, which is much more far-fetched, it seems to me, than that of either the Trotskyites or the Soviet Union itself. First of all he objects to the term Stalinism, which he thinks is somehow both a Trotskyite and a bourgeois liberal conception. He wants to replace this term by what he calls the 'Stalinian deviation'. Secondly, and this is again somewhat obscure, instead of saying that Stalinism is a mistake, he says the essential fault of Stalinism is the failure to *recognize* the mistake. The answer to this is that had they read more of Lenin and Marx, then they would have recognized sooner that they had made a mistake. The extraordinary climax to Althusser's explanation is to say that actually Stalinism was a fault of the Second International, not the Third. What he actually says is that Stalinism is perhaps the secret revenge of the Second International on the Third, and that the main crime that Stalin was guilty of was 'economism'. I'll leave you to mull over how convincing you find that as an explanation... The more serious and fundamental point that it raises is the difficulty, from a Leninist perspective (and I would include Trotskyism within a Leninist perspective in this sense) of actually being able to provide an adequate representation of what in principle was 'un-Leninist' about Stalinist practice.

The Language of the 60s

The next point I want to make is simply that a lot of the appeal of Althusser, his intellectual appeal in the 1960s, came from the way in which he managed brilliantly to redescribe Marxism in the language of the 1960s — particularly that of structuralism, but also using Freudian psychoanalysis, the Freudian theory of the unconscious as a way of somehow reposing the problem of the relationship between the economic and other instances of a social formation; and the use of a Bachelardian theory of science to establish the scientificity of *Capital* and so on. This, of course, was very important in attracting an intelligentsia towards the French Communist Party, or at least around it, at a time when for many other reasons they might have been in the intellectual doldrums.

But it is again worth noting that for Althusser, himself, it was Leninism rather than structuralism that was important. It was because he was aware that the intellectual landscape in France was dominated by structuralist fashions, that Althusser found ways of re-expressing classical Marxist and Leninist themes in the language of structuralism. An example of this is the distinction he makes between real objects and the objects of knowledge — a distinction central to much structuralist discourse in the 1960s. It is worth recalling that when Althusser came to write his self-criticism — and self-criticism is perhaps not the best word here — he confessed that what he was doing was not so much *being* a structuralist, as *using* certain structuralist terms to present a position which had originally, philosophically speaking, come from Spinoza. To remind you that Spinoza also had an ancestry in Russian and Leninist Marxism, I should mention that Plekhanov, often called the 'father of Russian Marxism' actually went all the way to London in 1889 to ask Engels this question: In your opinion was Spinoza right in saying that thought and extension are only two attributes of a single substance? Certainly, Engels replied, Spinoza was entirely right.

You shouldn't think when you read Althusser, that what is at question is some kind of parroting of the structuralist concepts fashionable in the 1960s. That may sometimes be the surface appearance of Althusser's texts. Beneath it however, lies an entrenched Leninist vision of society, sustained by a lineage of concepts deriving from Russian Marxism rather than simply Marx himself. It is worth remembering in this context that Hegel thought he had put 'Spinoza on wheels'; that is to say, that he had introduced a teleology and historical process into what was otherwise a rather static confrontation between the real order of things and the order of thought. Historically, there is no doubt that Marx's thought developed out of that of Hegel, rather than that of Spinoza. So it is interesting — and a measure of the extent of Althusser's theoretical ambition — that he rediscovered, not only Lenin, but also some of the sources of Lenin's theory and Lenin's philosophical inspiration, a tradition of Russian Marxism in which Spinoza had played a primordial role.

I would like to conclude by suggesting some sort of historical explanation for the phenomenon of Althusser and the cluster of preoccupations and self-conceptions which characterised French theoretical Marxism between the 1940s and the 1970s. Here I think it is necessary to step back from the much publicised theoretical disagreements between Sartre and Althusser and to focus upon the more general issues which historically bound them together. For since we are dealing with a movement of ideas which ended in such a visible collapse, it is worth asking what it was that had sustained its authority and credibility for so long.

In the end the rise and fall of post-war French Marxism

would seem to have as much to do with the political history
of France as the history of the international communist
movement or the history of marxist theory per se. The
formative moment of this kind of thought dates back to 1940,
to the collapse — moral as well as military — of the Third
Republic, to the institution of the Vichy regime and to the
choice between collaboration and resistance. These events
dominated the subsequent outlook of the intellectual generation of which Sartre was such a powerful and prolific spokes-
man. France's experience of the Second World War, the facts
of occupation and collaboration or resistance, bequeathed a
cold war in French public life. 1940 had discredited the Third
Republic in practice and its legitimacy remained very weak in
the fifteen years after the Second World War. In such a
situation, the only parties which were in a position to compete in the formation of a new definition of national identity
were the Communists and the Gaullists. A few French intellectuals, most notably Malraux, attempted to elaborate an
ideology of Gaullism; but for most, De Gaulle was a suspect
figure, because of the Bonapartist or Boulangist connota-
tions of Gaullist politics. Most gravitated towards the left,
where the Communist Party — the Party of the resistance
and hence the inheritor of the mantle of revolutionary repub-
licanism — represented the continuation of that resistance,
not only to Fascism but also to the idea of a France subordin-
ated to an American-dominated western alliance. The fact
that the Party was not only the Party of the Resistance, but
had also become the Party of the working class, and that it
was not difficult to establish intimate associations between
Jacobinism and Leninism, meant that it became the symbol
of heroism, integrity and the revolutionary tradition. To
have scrutinised too closely the day-to-day Stalinist practices
of the Party would have risked dismantling the mythological
structure which sustained its prestige. Thus the distanceless
distance between the intelligentsia and the Party constructed
by Sartre and Merleau Ponty, and reproduced under more
extraordinary circumstances from within Party ranks by
Althusser, established a collusive relationship between communism and the intellectuals, apparently impervious to outside developments in socialist countries. The most important
fact about the French Communist Party was not its day to
day political practices, but its intransigence, its preservation

in different circumstances of a frozen moment of existential choice and commitment dating from 1940. I think it is from this very Manichean vision of either total commitment to something, or else, as Sartre says, to nothingness, that the most salient contours of French marxist discussion are to be understood, right through from the foundation of *Temps Modernes* by Sartre and Merleau Ponty to the end of Althusser's public career and the suicide of Poulantzas — events which brought this whole train of thought to its term.

Total commitment to resistance became total commitment to the cause of the working class in post-war France. And between the actual French working class and the marxist-leninist vision of the proletariat represented by the Communist Party, intellectuals like Sartre, and after him, Althusser, were prepared to make little or no distinction. It is this sort of equation between Party and class which explained much of the apparent credulity towards Communism and Stalinism expressed in different ways by Sartre and Althusser. To deny Communism, said Sartre, 'it is necessary that the proletariat as a whole is either criminal, a liar or hysteric. If not, how can one explain that it remains communist? If the working class wishes to detach itself from the Party, that is nothing but a means of its falling into dust'. Or again — this is Althusser: 'when a working class party tends to abandon the principles of class independence in its political practice, it tends to reproduce in its own bosom the practice of bourgeois politics'.

In other words, what is set up by this problematic is the belief that the proletariat only exists as the Communist Party and that the Communist Party is the only historically authentic expression of the proletariat. Without that, it has no empirical existence, it simply dissolves into dust. This, I think, provides some explanation of the peculiarly tortured relationship between these major intellectuals and a Party, which by any standards was pretty rigid and unimaginative in its practice of French politics between the 40s and the 60s.

I think 1968 already represented the end of Althusserianism. Two decades after 1945, French society was no longer polarised by the issues which had surfaced at the beginning of the Second World War. The choice was no longer between Communism and Fascism. Economic prosperity and a period of political stability had begun to undermine the appeal of a disciplined Leninist Party. The prevalent mood of the student left in 1968 was libertarian rather than marxist and for the first time Althusserianism was put to the test of practical politics in the context of a new France which had grown up since the Second World War, and for whom Vichy was not even a memory. In this situation, Althusser could do no more than argue that students were petit bourgeois dupes. He could discern no positive meaning in the May events. Moreover, the peremptory ending of the Prague spring by Soviet invasion put the question of Stalinism again at the centre of the agenda of the intellectual left. How a French socialism, let alone a French Communism might avoid Stalinism was a question which could no longer be kept at bay. In 1974 the dam broke with the publication of the *Gulag Archipelago*. After three decades of evasion of the problems of Stalinism on the part of the most influential spokesmen of the French intelligentsia, what had been repressed returned in the most brutal and destructive fashion, bringing down in its train most of the problematic within which French intellectual Marxists had worked. In a narrow sense, it was a nemesis, not wholly undeserved, but its larger and more unfortunate effect has been to put an end to virtually all forms of creative marxist thought in France.

POST-STRUCTURALIST CRITIQUES OF MARXISM AND THE CONTRADICTIONS OF ALTHUSSER
Ted Benton

The tide of opinion among intellectuals in France today is running strongly against Marxism. This is in marked contrast to any comparable episode since the end of the World War II. During this post-war period, French intellectual life has been dominated by Marxism, and France's Marxist philosophers — most notably Sartre, Merleau-Ponty and Althusser himself — have been amongst the most widely influential of all 20th century Marxist thinkers. No doubt this fact is linked with the presence in France of one of the most powerful Communist Parties and Trade Union movements in Europe, as well as the legacy of war-time resistance to Nazism, in which the Communists played so decisive a part.

But this pervasive influence of Marxism in French intellectual life is not without its paradoxes when viewed in the context of Communist organisation and politics. Neither Sartre nor Merleau-Ponty (whose alignment with Marxism was, in any case, short-lived) took their interest in Marxism to the point of Party membership, and neither found Marxism to be intellectually self-sufficient. On the contrary, for them Marxism stood in need of outside help from other philosophies if it was to fulfil its emancipatory promise. Though much more generally misunderstood and misrepresented, Althusser's philosophical work is similarly ambiguous in its relation to both the intellectual heritage of the classics of Marxism, and to its organisational presence in French politics. Despite his self-professed 'orthodoxy', Althusser borrowed (guardedly, and somewhat shamefacedly, it is true) from French conventionalist epistemology and philosophy of science, from structuralism, and from psychoanalysis. In politics, though a member of the

Communist Party, Althusser has been, viewed from the stand-point of the Party leadership, at best an awkward and prob-lematic presence in the Party, at worst an articulate and forceful opponent.

The ambiguity in the relationship of these French intellec-tuals to Marxism (in both its theoretical and practical forms) can, I think, be understood in terms of the paradoxical charac-ter of Marxism itself. It is, on the one hand, a discourse which has sustained countless resistances and revolts against oppres-sion. Third-World peasants, industrial workers of Europe, Latin America, Asia and Africa, feminists in many countries, oppressed ethnic minorities, and many others have thought and spoken the language of Marxism as a way of articulating their protest, and formulating their strategies. At the same time, some of the most pervasive, durable systems of social domination witnessed in the 20th century were created in the name of Marxism, and continue to be legitimated through its terms.

For intellectuals in post-war France the dominant significa-tion of adherance to Marxism was its aspect as discourse of revolt, resistance and liberation. But its other dimenion was nonetheless present — the commitment to Marxism was for many, less than whole-hearted. For the 'second generation' of post-war French Marxist intellectuals, of whom Althusser is by far the best known, it was characteristic to be attracted by the apparently quite different strand of Marxism being de-veloped in China and Vietnam, to be in tension with the PCF leadership, and, after 1968, to leave the Party altogether.

For these Marxists, 'structuralist' no less than 'humanist', the aim was to 'de-Stalinise' Marxism — to rescue the authen-ticity of the tradition from its deformation or degeneration, or alternatively to renew its liberatory potential by fusion with other philosophies. Against this quest for a renewed, authentic, genuinely liberatory Marxism the new wave of 'post-structuralist' and post-Marxist critics insists that Marxism is in its *essence* a totalitarian project: nothing less than the complete abandonment of Marxism as such is required. My own view is that their diagnosis and the associated prescription is dis-astrously mistaken. At the same time, I think that it would be equally disastrous for Marxists to underestimate the force of the critical case. The authoritarian historical legacy of Marxism is no mere aberration or distortion — it is, indeed, deeply rooted in even the classic writings of Marx and Engels. If a political practice which is both democratic and emancipatory is to be built, it will have to be built on the rejection of some quite fundamental theoretical and strategic precepts which have been inherited from the 'founding fathers'. But to say this is still to be a very long way from those who call for a root-and-branch rejection of Marxism.

It is to the arguments of these critics that I now turn. I shall do this by taking three themes from the work of Althusser. In each case, Althusser's work is a *target* of post-structuralist attacks, yet, at the same time, the critics use weapons which they also *derive* from Althusser and other structural Marxists. To a considerable extent, the relationship between structural Marxism and its critics consists in the exploitation of unresolved tensions in the former. One aspect, or tendency, of structuralism is abstracted and elaborated only to be deployed against another. In this respect, structural Marxism and post-structuralism may be held to move within a closed circle of ideas. As I shall try to show, opening that circle is a necessary condition for developing the kind of democratic and liberatory discourse which was the aim of both Althusser and Poulantzas as well as some of their post-structuralist critics.

Science and Rationality

In an interview published as recently as 1983, Foucault commented that a guiding thread in his work had been an examination of the conditions under which it had been made possible, in the West, to 'tell the truth' about oneself. Foucault's diverse writings, on the history of the asylum and the modern prison system, his history of sexuality and his archaeology of the human sciences, despite the sometimes quite radical shifts of perspective and approach, can, indeed, all be seen as linked by such a threat. Each can be seen as a *particular* positing of questions as to the social-relational conditions for the emergence of specific forms of knowledge, and, centrally, those knowledges in which the human subject takes itself as a possible object of scientific knowledge. Foucault's more recent work, specially *Discipline and Punish*, and *History of Sexuality*, Vol. 1, were more explicit in their assertion that these social-relational conditions are relations of power – the vestments of strategies of domination. Each project for a human science is understood or inscribed within a power-relation which both produces knowledge as its effect andn also establishes knowledge itself as a *technique* of power.

Foucault's displacement, in the analysis of forms of discourse, of epistemic questions of truth and falsity, in favour of questions of power, interests and strategies is an important element in the wider post-structuralist subversion of the Enlightenment project of liberation through science, knowledge and reason. For the Enlightenment, ignorance, obscurantism and mysticism were enemies of progress; truth, reason and science its indispensible prerequisites.

For the post-structuralists these are merely the slogans of a new, more systematic, more totalising, and so more deadly modern power-play. And if Marxism presents itself as the apex of this post-Enlightenment quest for a human science, and defends its claims to knowledge with the very latest philosophies of science, then it is but a short step from Foucault's careful genealogies to the more direct and challenging question: Within what strategy of power or domination is Marxism-as-science inscribed? Will not the most rigorous, universal and rational of the human sciences be the instrument of the most rigorous, universal and rational systems of domination yet devised?

This, then, is one direct route to an understanding of Marxism, the self-proclaimed 'science' of history, as inherently and essentially oppressive. Indeed, viewed from this perspective, Marxism is oppressive in a way which is systematic, all-inclusive and formidable to a degree so far unattained by the 'disciplinary' regimes and bureaucratic state administrations of the West. Marxism heralds, it can be made to seem, not a revolutionary break with modern capitalist industrial rationality, but rather the furthest extrapolation and fullest development of its totalitarian potential. As Foucault seemed to acknowledge, there is a striking parallel between this critique of Marxism as embodying and augmenting a certain peculiarly Western form of rationality, and the critique of socialism developed in the early years of this century by the sociologist Max Weber.

Since the structural Marxism of Althusser and his associates is clearly the principal target of this critique, let us see how accurately it is aimed. Paradoxically, whilst it is true that epistemology was a major preoccupation in much of Althusser's work, and that 'scientificity' became the watchword of a whole generation of Marxists influenced by it, it is also true that the tradition of structural Marxism spectacularly failed to resolve the central epistemological tension with which it was beset. Put simply, this tension derives from Althusser's simultaneous commitment to a materialist view of knowledge as a relationship between thought and an external reality which exists prior to and independently of the thinker, and to a view of science as a historically transient social practice. The source of the former view is in the dialectical materialist classics of Engels and Lenin, and of the latter in French conventionalist philosophy of science and the 'historical epistemology' of Gaston Bachelard. The former view is required by Althusser not simply to guarantee this 'orthodoxy' within the Marxist tradition, but more centrally to sustain the *critical* cutting edge of his 'reading' of Marx against its opponents: science and ideology, truth and falsity, have to be opposed in the clearest possible terms. The latter, 'conventionalist' view of science, as a social practice and product is necessary in providing the means to analyse and historically periodise Marx's works. This view of science is the source of Althusser's notorious proclamation of an 'epistemological break' in Marx's work.

Now this second view of science is really quite close to Foucault's — indeed, it rises from the same sources — and Althusser was not afraid, on occasion, to represent the 'epistemological break' in Marx's work as itself the product of social and political causes. Even in the earlier 'theoreticist' writings, Althusser speaks of knowledge as a practice of production, with definite relations of production. Since, for Marxists, production relations are, in essence, relations of power it seems that little, if anything separates Althusser from his poststructuralist critics. But, of course, this appearance is deceptive. For all this later self-criticism and revisions Althusser never followed Foucault in displacing questions of truth and falsity of course in favour of the epistemically non-committal genealogical or archaeological tracing of the conditions and effects of particular cognitive discourses: the question of the truth or falsity of knowledge-claims remains, for Althusser, independent of questions as to the interests at stake in their constitution or the effects of their deployment.

To attempt to sustain both the idea of truth and falsity as correspondence/non-correspondence to external reality and the idea of knowledge as socially constituted is not the same thing as coherently to reconcile the two perspectives, or aspects of the theory of knowledge. It was this latter prospect which systematically eluded Althusser. In the absence of a satisfactory synthesis, the way was open to two opposed and one-sided resolutions of the tension. First, a rationalist way out. This is to take the basic concepts of historical materialism, as 'given' by an authoritative reading of the classics of the tradition, and to treat these concepts as *synthetic a priori* conditions of all possible knowledge of society. At best such a resolution reduces Marxist intellectual work to a laborious and sterile. exercise in social taxonomy and 'conceptual-policing'; at worst it can legitimate the dogmatic and authoritarian imposition of the 'reason' of the Party-intellectual upon the 'experience' of the 'subjects' it mobilises and controls. It is this one-sided resolution of the epistemological tension of Althussian Marxism, then, that does, indeed, give credence to the post-structuralist critique.

But there is a second, equally one-sided possible resolution of the tension — this time, in a 'conventionalist' direction. This route countenances the abandonment of epistemic considerations, and so of any opposition between truth and falsity, science and ideology. 'Science' is to be studied as one socially-constituted discourse among others, without favour or special privilege. This was, in fact, the route taken by Rancière, among others. When turned back upon Marxism itself as a 'science', then it generates the familiar post-structuralist critique of Marxism. The critique and its object are but elaborations of the opposite terms of the epistemological contradiction of structural Marxism.

At this stage, I shall restrict myself to three comments on this epistemological theme in the critique of Marxism. First, the post-structuralist critique of Marxism as a rational technology of social domination is in a paradoxical way far too generous to Marxism — it takes as redeemed some of the more extravagant promises of rationalist Marxism. Few serious Marxists would share such confidence in the cognitive achievements of their tradition. Second, the 'anti-scientism' of much post-structuralist thinking again concedes far too much to scientism itself. Only if the scientist equation of science with rationality and rationality with technical domination and bureaucratic order is left unquestioned is it possible to see science and reason as unequivocal enemies of liberty. The science/domination complex is a technicist distortion of the idea of scientific knowledge, which grossly oversimplifies and caricatures the balance-sheet of modern science in relation to human welfare.

My third comment is that neither the dogmatising 'rationalist' resolution of structural Marxism's epistemological problems, nor their ultimately paracidal 'conventionalist' revolution is an adequate response to the original problem. That problem — how to reconcile a conception of truth or falsity as correspondence/non-correspondence to external reality with a notion of science as a social process — is simply evaded or denied in these strategies. The joint failure of structural Marxism and its critics in the face of this problem does not derive from any intrinsic incompatibility between these views or aspects of science, but from conceptual limitations shared by the two traditions. These conceptual limitations are twofold. First, an inability seriously to investigate the point played by 'experience' in the formation and correction of scientific thought - an inability largely determined by a bizarre and inappropriate critique of empiricism. Second, an isolation of French Marxism from other traditions of thought, such as Critical Theory, which has more sophisticated (but also, of course, still problematic) ways of understanding the relationships between rationality, science and technique; and scientific realism and critical rationalism, which offer views of science that integrate epistemic and social/historical dimensions.

State, Power and Party

Here, again, Foucault will be our starting-point. Though he denied that a 'theory of power' was any part of his intellectual project, Foucault's central concern with the relation between power and knowledge makes this claim hard to take very seriously. According to Foucault's analyses, 'discipline' is the peculiarly modern mode of operation of power. It produces a precision, specificity, reliability and pervasiveness in the regulation of individual behaviour which is not obtainable by either exemplary terror or by mere incarceration. Through the metaphor of the panopticon, Foucault indicates that it is by isolation and continuous surveillance that the 'subject' of modern society is 'subjected' as a self-monitoring, self-disciplining, autonomously subjected subject. This distinctive mode of operation of power is such that power is dispersed throughout the social body, to form what Foucault calls a 'microphysics' of power, that 'goes right down to the depths of society'. It follows that 'power' is not, as the Marxist classics had always taught, concentrated in certain central state institutions — the coercive apparatuses of the state. It is, rather, produced in a whole complex of impersonal institutions and reaches into the inner-self of each individual. Neither is power the 'possession' of the ruling class but, rather, as Foucault puts it, 'the overall effect of its strategic positions'.

At stake in this view of power as dispersed throughout society is the whole Leninist strategy of social transformation by way of a 'proletarian' capture of state power. If the power of the old class is diffused right down to the depths of society and is present in the very self-disciplining subjectivity of its subjects, then a mere transfer of state power will leave all this untouched. The consequence, a necessary escalation in the perfection of the dictatorship of the proletariat, and the transformation of it into a dictatorship *over* the proletariat — delaying for ever the promised 'withering away' of the state. Paradoxically, other post-structuralists take an absolutely opposite view of the relation between power and the modern state. For them, the overriding threat to the liberty of the subject is the increasing concentration of power in the form of a monolithic state. But the critique of Marxism is the same: its mission is to complete the trajectory of increasingly oppressive and centralised state power which has characterised the West in the modern period.

Again, the post-structuralist critiques are not unambiguously applicable to Althusser and his associates. This has something to do with unresolved tensions in structural Marxism itself. Althusser's view of strategy was in essence a Leninist one, but his political thought also took much from Gramsci, and was variably influenced by the cultural and political stances of the post-'68 left. This was still more true of some of his one-time associates, such as Balibar, Rancière and Poulantzas. In the work of Althusser, there is the famous distinction between the ideological and the repressive state apparatuses, and the insistence upon the 'relative autonomy' of the superstructures. There is, too, an insistence on the significance of non-class forms of struggle such as those of women and 'youth'. These ideas could have opened the way in Althusser - for others they *did* open the way — to conceptions of diverse, decentralised modes of struggle against the existing order as a new strategic option. But even in his most bitter denunciations of the Party leadership in the later 1970s, Althusser still protested against the abuse of democratic centralism, rather than against centralism itself. I know of no evidence that he ever broke from the view of the PCF as a vanguard party which would centralise and direct the diverse struggles of which he was aware, and to which he was — to a degree — attentive.

I think the key to this instability in Althusser's thought is the inability to give real theoretical content to the phrase 'relative autonomy'. If the determining power of the economic structure is exercised only in 'the last instance', and the last instance never comes, as Althusser once remarked, then the way is open to an analysis of specific ideological and political processes and struggles *as if* they were *absolutely* autonomous with respect to any overall pattern of power in society. A Foucauldian indefinite dispersal of power 'to the depth of society' is quite compatible with such a reading of Althusser. But, of course, such a reading of Althusser would have to abstract, onesidedly, from texts such as the famous 'I.S.As' ('Ideology and Ideological State Apparatuses') essay, which comes close to a rigidly functionalist interpretation of base, superstructure, and the reproduction of class-power. In texts such as these, 'relative autonomy' shrinks to the status of a thin veil to cover the nakedness of class domination.

But if Althusser failed to provide us with a coherent 'anatomy' of power in contemporary capitalist societies, the failure of his critics is still more pronounced. Neither Foucault nor the so-called 'New Philosophers' have attempted a serious analysis which could sustain an effective oppositional political movement. Power is either indifferently diffused through society, so that no strategic priorities could be identified, or it is centralised in such a way that forces of resistance could never challenge it without themselves becoming a new, and more oppressive centre of power.

Certainly, Foucault recognised as an inseparable 'other

face' of power, a necessary spontaneous heritage, but the social diffusion of power is such that this could be no more than a localised, marginal, unorganised affair. For resistance to become more than this, for it to become an organised challenge to the prevailing order of society would be for 'resistance' to transform itself into yet another 'strategy of power', policing and subjecting those it mobilised. The impossibiity of an emancipatory movement is not the pessimistic result of Foucault's analysis, but rather it is written into the very conceptual structure of his discourse on power. Neither Althusser nor Foucault, much less the New Philosophers, were able to develop a conception of social power as 'productive of effects' yet at the same time not a form of domination.

Ideology and Subjectivity

Here again, we can distinguish more than one 'post-structuralist' route to a critique of Marxism as a form of domination. Writers such as Deleuze, Lyotard and others have developed the familiar view that the 'rationalisation' of modern Western economic, cultural and political life has been achieved at the cost of an enormous libidinal sacrifice on the part of the individual 'subject'. In this perspective, Marxism in its continuity with this Western rationalising project, is merely the most recent and highly developed form of 'policing' of the social order. It represents power, order and reason, against disorder, desire and rebellion. There is, too, a 'feminist' version of this thematic argument — it is to see in the rationality of Marxism but the continuation of the specifically patriarchal rationality of Western social domination, and so to identify the interests of women with a non-rational libidinal rebellion against Marxist and bourgeois culture, as both indifferently patriarchal. Undoubtedly, these argumentative moves do give an initially plausible way of interpreting the puritanism of some Marxist regimes, as well as the 'policing' and recuperative role of the PCF in relation to the revolutionary workers and students of May 1968.

But this is far from Foucault's position. His *History of Sexuality* (Vol. 1) is a sustained critique of what he calls the 'repressive hypothesis', and, by implication, the (rather loosely!) Freudian underpinnings of much of the work of the 'philosophers of desire'. The theme, widespread in attempts to link Marxism with psychoanalysis, that the institutional repression required as a condition of capitalist economic and social life may provide both the moral foundation and the motivational dynamic for anti-capitalist struggles, is opposed by Foucault. This Freudian-Marxist perspective shares with the 'philosophers of desire' a vision of emancipation in a libidinally expressive society. Foucault's analysis, by contrast, results in a view of sexuality itself, like subjecthood (with which, of course, it is intimately linked), as constituted by a strategy of power. Power is productive, not simply repressive, and, among other things, it has produced a whole inventory of discourses upon sexuality. And if subjecthood and sexuality are constituted as tactics in a strategy of power, how can they simultaneously be the means of resistance to power, much less the content of an adequate vision of liberation from it?

So it seems that our sexuality and our very identity as self-conscious subjects, far from resources and objects of liberatory practice are, on the contrary, the lived forms of our subjection, the products of elaborate mechanisms of domination. How, then, is resistance possible? Both Foucault and the 'philosophers of desire' seem to think it *is* possible, so how and in what form? In the form, it seems, of a direct, spontaneous, inarticulate and non-rational unleashing of the libido, in the case of the 'philosophers of desire', or, in the case of Foucault, in the shape of an unspecified recovery of the 'pleasures of the body'.

A precisely parallel inability to give content to emancipatory or socilaist strategy in terms of subjective experience is to be found in the work of Althusser. And, again, this inability has its source in an inner conceptual tension in his work. Both Althusser and Foucault have in common with the wider structuralist tradition an opposition to 'subject-centred' views of social order. Of course, to reject the claims of the 'constitutive subject' is not necessarily to adopt a view of subjecthood as wholly constituted — but all too often both Althusser and Foucault fall into this naive inversion of philoshical 'humanism'. For Althusser as for Foucault,to be a *subject* is to be *subjected*. Subjecthood is the form in which social subjection is lived. The strategic consequences of this identification in Althusser's work are notoriously well-rehearsed. Ideology is the 'lived relation' of 'subjects' to their conditions of existence, and is to be sharply distinguished from 'science', which gives us a *knowledge* of those conditions of existence. If this is so, strategic priorities must be handed down by the Party-authorities, even where this overrides the 'lived experience' of the constituted 'subjects' of the (dominant) ideology who are directed and mobilised by the Party.

Here, it seems, in Althusser's theory of ideology and subjectivity, is the confirmation of the oppressive, 'policing' function which the 'philosophers of desire' attribute to Marxism. But there is another side to Althusser, most apparent in his increasingly bitter denunciations of the PCF leadership in the late 1970s, in which he called upon it to be 'attentive to the powers of imagination and invention of the masses'. And this is no momentary outburst, unrelated to the deeper framework of Althusser's thought. The notion of *ideological struggle* as a specific practice within the complex totality of class struggle was always insisted upon by Althusser, but the failure fully to break from the identification of subjectivity with subjection, and therefore of ideology with ruling ideology cut him off from developing a conception of genuinely diverse and democratic mass struggle.

But neither Foucault nor the philosophers of desire have succeeded where Althusser failed. If we follow them we seem to be confined to visions of resistance as spontaneous, diverse, inarticulate and libidinal, and, at least in the case of Foucault, to a denial of the liberatory content in the ideas of personal and sexual autonomy or expression. For all the power of their case against one face of Althusser's structural Marxism, the post-structuralists remain entrapped within a unilateral perspective on the 'constitution' of subjectivity and sexuality. Just as there is no *necessity* in the identification of knowledge with science, nor yet of science with instrumental reason, nor, again, in the identification of power with domination, so there is no necessity in the identification of subjectivity with subjection. Practices of struggle provide conditions which actors transform and enlarge their subjective world in ways which may provide both resources for further struggle and contents for their liberatory ideal. The idea of an 'oppositional subjectivity' is close to a contradiction-in-terms not only for Althusser, but also for Foucault and other post-structuralists. The peculiarly Western forms of individualism and self-reflective subjectivity, as well as the sexual politics of recent decades have a complex and ambiguous balance sheet, but they are so deeply constitutive of current forms of political action and thought in the West that it is hard to see how any emancipatory vision could be seriously sustained without them. Certainly, the forms of abandonment of those projects of personal and libidinal emancipation implicit in Foucault and the philosophers of desire seem particularly unpromising; a vague appeal to bodily pleasure in the first case, an apparently mindless and cultureless libidinal gratification in the second.

References

L. Althusser, *For Marx*, London, 1969.

L. Althusser, *Lenin and Philosophy and Other Essays*, London, 1971.

L. Althusser, *Essays in Self-Criticism*, London, 1976.

L. Althusser, translated essays in *New Left Review*, Nos. 104 and 109.

T. Benton, *The Rise and Fall of Structural Marxism*, London and Basingstoke, 1984.

A. Callinicos, *Is There a Future for Marxism?* London and Basingstoke, 1982.

G. Deleuze and F. Guattari, *Anti-Oedipus*, New York, 1977.

V. Descombes, *Modern French Philosophy*, Cambridge, 1980.

P. Dews, 'Power and Subjectivity in Foucault', *New Left Review*, 144, March/April, 1984.

M. Foucault, *Discipline and Punish*, London, 1977.

M. Foucault, *History of Sexuality*, Vol. 1, London, 1981.

M. Foucault, (ed. C. Gordon), *Power and Knowledge*, Brighton, 1980.

A. Glucksmann, *The Master-Thinkers*, Brighton, 1980.

J. Ranciere, 'On the Theory of Ideology', *Radical Philosophy*, No. 7, Spring 1974.

G. Roulet, 'Structuralism and Post-Structuralism: An Interview with Michel Foucault', *Telos*, 55, Spring 1983.

ALTHUSSER AND THE CONCEPT OF IDEOLOGY
Michèle Barrett

My remarks are restricted to the specific question of Louis Althusser's use of the concept of ideology, and my focus will be on the influence of his work in Britain. I want to argue that Althusser posed, though did not himself solve, the central problem that concerns theories of ideology and this is why his work is still of great relevance and importance. I believe that this unresolved problem in Althusser's use of the concept of ideology corresponds with the major current bifurcation in work around ideology. What is this problem? I want to go back to the well-known essay 'Ideology and Ideological State Apparatuses', written in 1969 and published in English in 1971[1]. It was an essay that fell into two entirely separate sections:—

i) In the first part Althusser gave an analysis of the ideological state apparatuses in terms of the concept of reproduction of the social relations of production. He argued that state repression is complemented by ideological processes ensuring capitalist reproduction through, most notably, school and family, but also through the church, the legal system, the political parties, trades unions, media, the arts and so on. These ideologies express class positions and are determined by them (if relatively autonomously). Although this argument was extensively criticized as functionalist, it has proved extremely influential, particularly in the analysis of education, domestic labour, the media and so on.

ii) In the second part Althusser offers a theory of ideology, as opposed to an analysis of ideologies, seeing ideology as 'a representation of the imaginary relationship of individuals to their real conditions of existence'. As such ideology has no history, and Althusser argues that it operates through the interpellation (hailing) of individuals as subjects. This constitutes recognition. When Althusser writes 'Disappeared: the term *ideas*. Survive: the terms *subject, consciousness, belief, actions*', it is easy to see why the second part of the essay should have attracted such attention as a solution to the undoubted problems of reductionist or humanist theories of ideology.

The choice between the two parts of the essay seemed to be between seeing ideology as an agent of the reproduction of the class relations of capitalism, and seeing it as a key to the understanding of subjectivity as an important question in its own right.

A comparable way of posting this dichotomy is to look, as Jorge Larrain does, at ideology in terms of a fundamental split between those who follow Marx in insisting on the critical (class partial) definition of ideology and those who follow Lenin (as well as many liberal sociologists) in regarding ideology more neutrally as the consciousness of historically specific classes. Larrain argues that Althusser himself is ambiguous on this, and this is the source of 'a division of the Althusser field' into those who retain a critical perspective on ideology and those who see ideology as the construction of subjectivities whose class affiliations are not pre-given. It might be noted here that both sides follow Althusser in rejecting the problematic of false-consciousness.[2]

'Ideology and Ideological State Apparatuses'

'Ideology and Ideological State Apparatuses' has been subjected to an exhaustive critique in the years since it appeared. Perhaps the most comprehensive is Terry Eagleton's footnote describing it as simultaneously 'functionalist, economistic, technicist, structuralist and idealist', though nonetheless 'really quite suggestive'.[3] The ambivalence of this formulation is symptomatic of the tension about Francophilia that is relevant to any account of the reception of Althusser's work in Britain. In 1979 Stuart Hall saw a tendency in 'vulgar Althusserianism' towards an 'abject and supine dependence on anything, provided it was written in French'.[4] Today it is a different French language that is of interest to the British intellectual avant-garde and the imports of Althusser and his era are regarded as of merely historical significance. Hence Ted Benton can entitle his book *The Rise and Fall of Althusserian Marxism* and Gareth StedmanJones has declared that 1968 was Althusser's epitaph. Yet these reports of death are, as they say, exaggerations. Far from Althusser being theoretically dead, I would argue that the dominant trends in work on ideology in Britain throughout the seventies and early eighties have been profoundly influenced by his work. Here I want briefly to mention what seem to me to be the major areas of work in this area in relation to Althusser's concept of ideology.

The lines of development from the above-mentioned essay I would place in two main summary categories, following the divided concerns mentioned above.

i) Work using the reproduction thesis — the first part of the essay — most profitably in cultural studies, analysis of the education system, of the family and also of the media. The problem of functionalism arises immediately in relation to this type of work, then that of tending to see language as transparent. Also, given that family/gender questions were central to some appropriations of the reproduction thesis, a further problem is that of how to reconcile an independent concern with gender with Althusser's own exclusive concern with agencies such as the family in terms of the reproduction of class relations.

ii) The main post-Althusserian tendency in this area has been the increasing importance attached to questions of language and of subjectivity, and (for some) the relation between them. Here Althusser, in the second part of the essay, paved the way for the substantial rise of interest in semiotics and signification, and the immense interest in Barthes, as well as for the particular stress on gendered subjectivity developed in relation to Lacan. Surprising though it may be to some, signification theory is probably now a consensual (compromise?) position in cultural studies and radical criticism — it is regarded as neither reductionist nor idealist. (Ideology is understood as inscribed in material practices of signification.) Some of this work undoubtedly corrects earlier prob-

lems, but perhaps the most general difficulty with it in terms
of the concept of ideology is that it leaves open (undertheo-
rized) the relation between language or sign and other
dimensions of the social formation. Obviously there are
many exceptions here (for example Pecheux's study of how
the right comes to dominate left discourse[5], but the overriding problem is, I think, a tendency to take specificity too
far. Equally we should not forget that when Althusser spoke
of the subject he referred explicitly to the ambiguity of the
term — subjectivity but also *subjection* to authority.

(Paradoxically a third school of thought — the one usually
called 'post-Althusserianism' — is in my view the least indebted to Althusser, whom it has decisively rejected. Discourse
theory's rejection of the classic theory of representation, of
the notion of social totality, its rejection of any form of
determination take it beyond the paradigm of ideology. This
is beyond the scope of the present discussion.)

The first and second developments I have mentioned reflect the division in Althusser's essay, and his attempt to
reconcile them through the concept of 'misrecognition',
which he ties very closely to class-generated forms of misrecognition, comes too late in the essay to convince. Before any
such reconciliation were to emerge, and from a materialist
point of view it would be a desirable development, it would
need to address many problems — of which I mention only
two:—

a) The question of humanism and the individual. Here stem a
series of questions about experience and agency that were
evaded in the concept of 'bearer', but are now rejected
wholesale in favour of preoccupations about pleasure and
desire that are as yet difficult to formulate in an anti-
humanist discourse.[6]

b)The question of class, and forms of non-class domination.
For example, Paul Willis (in his book on 'how working class
kids get working class jobs') gives us a brilliant and user-
friendly version of the reproduction thesis — but in his
persuasive account of the deal done between masculine privilege and the exploitation of manual labour, it is hard to see
whether we could apply the argument either to bourgeois or

white-collar men or to women.[7] In general the reproduction thesis is problematic when applied to gender — since Althusser couched it so firmly in a class analysis and the relation between class, race and gender is still untheorized.[8] Equally the vexed problem of tying a semiotic analysis to either class, race or gender exploitation or domination is resistant to an easy solution, though notable attempts have been made (such as Judith Williamson's work on advertising [9]).

Notes

1. Louis Althusser, *Lenin and Philosophy and Other Essays,* London, Verso 1977.
2. Jorge Larrain, *Marxism and Ideology,* London, Macmillan 1983.
3. Terry Eagleton, 'Ideology, Fiction, Narrative' in *Social Text,* Summer 1979, No. 2, pp 62-3.
4. Stuart Hall, 'In Defence of Theory' in *People's History and Socialist Theory,* ed. R. Samuel, London, RKP 1981, p380.
5. Reported in John B Thomson, *Studies in the Theory of Ideology,* Polity/Blackwell, 1984, p243.
6. This argument is elaborated further in my 'The Place of Aesthetics in Marxist Criticism' in *Marxism and the Interpretation of Culture,* ed C Nelson and L Grossberg, University of Illinois Press, (forthcoming).
7. Paul Willis, *Learning to Labour,* London, Saxon House 1977.
8. See my *Women's Oppression Today* (Ch 4) for an extended discussion of this problem. London, Verso 1980.
9. Judith Williamson *De-coding Advertisements,* London, Marion Boyars 1978.

THE NON-STRUCTURALIST LEGACY OF NICOS POULANTZAS
Bob Jessop

This colloquium is concerned with French structuralism and its current theoretical and political legacies in France. My task is to discuss the work of Poulantzas in this context. Unfortunately for such a division of labour, Poulantzas was never whole-heartedly committed to French structuralism, even in its Althusserian guise. Instead he was influenced by several intellectual traditions and attempted to integrate them into a new Marxist theory of the state. His theoretical influence in France has also waned with the rise of the irrationalism of the *nouveaux philosophes* whilst his political influence in France, always somewhat marginal, is more limited than ever. Rather than presenting Poulantzas as a structuralist *tout court*, therefore, I want to consider the complexities of his theoretical roots and their dynamic effect on his work. Likewise, rather than considering his impact on French politics, I want to consider the impact of French (and, more significant still, Greek) politics on Poulantzas.

The significance of Poulantzas

Five years after his tragic death on the 3 October 1979, why should one consider the work of Poulantzas? Why not focus on Marxist political theorists who are still active? Because Poulantzas was almost alone among postwar Marxists to address and answer the really crucial questions within Marxist politics. This can be seen by considering a recent critique of Western Marxism by one of its leading exponents.

Perry Anderson argues that Western Marxism has left unanswered the following key questions:

> What is the real nature and structure of *bourgeois democracy* as a type of State system, that has become the normal mode of

capitalist power in the advanced countries? What type of
revolutionary strategy is capable of overthrowing this historical form of State – so distinct from that of Tsarist Russia?
What would be the institutional forms of *socialist democracy*
in the West, beyond it? Marxist theory has scarcely touched
these three subjects in their interconnection. (Anderson,
1976, p 103)

But these three subjects in their interconnection are precisely the issues which concerned Poulantzas throughout his
tragically brief intellectual career. His first influential book,
Pouvoir politique et classes sociales (1968), was concerned
with the real nature and structure of bourgeois democracy.
Then *Fascisme et dictature* (1970) dealt with the nature of
fascist regimes and the failure of the labour movement to
check their rise or to overthrow them. It was also directly
concerned with the distinction between the 'normal mode of
capitalist power in the advanced countries' and various exceptional modes of bourgeois political domination. In this
third and fourth books, *Classes sociales dans le capitalisme
d'aujourd'hui* (1974) and *La Crise des dictatures* (1975),
Poulantzas related problems of revolutionary strategy to
democratic and exceptional regimes in both advanced and
dependent capitalist countries. And his final book, *L'Etat, le
pouvoir, le socialisme* discussed the current threats to
bourgeois democracy and the institutional forms which
socialist democracy might assume in the West. Moreover,
not only did Poulantzas tackle each of the three subjects
central to Marxist politics, he also discussed them increasingly in their interconnection.

If this were not enough, Poulantzas went beyond these
concerns to other important issues in Marxist theory. Here
again Anderson proves a useful guide since he mentions four
other failures of contemporary Marxism. It had not tackled
the meaning and position of the nation as a social unit and its
relationship to nationalism. It had ignored the contemporary
laws of motion of capitalism as a mode of production and the
forms of crisis specific to these laws. It had neglected the true
configuration of imperialism as an international system of
economic and political domination. And it had not confronted the nature of the bureaucratic states which arose in
those backward countries where socialist revolutions had
occurred. It would be too much to expect Poulantzas to have

tackled all these complex issues in the same detail and with the same rigour which he devoted to the capitalist state in the West. But he did deal with each of these issues to some extent. In particular he was concerned with contemporary imperialism and with the nature of modern capitalism as a system of political economy. He also touched on the nation and nationalism, bureaucratic socialism and Stalinism. In short he was an unusual Western marxist.

Marx and Poulantzas

The originality of Marx is often said to reside in his unique synthesis of the 'three sources of Marxism': German philosophy, French politics, and English economics. He was also influenced by quite specific political conditions and objectives. For he was not concerned merely with interpreting the world from his chair in the British Museum, but also with practical interventions to advance the cause of socialism. But this still does not explain how Marx was able to achieve this synthesis when others did not. Louis Althusser suggested that Marx's breakthrough occurred because he adopted an absolutely new, *proletarian* class position in both politics and philosophy. In particular Althusser argues that it was the change in philosophical position which secured the fundamental *precondition* of Marx's achievements in political economy. Without the politics, nothing would have happened. Without the philosophy of revolutionary materialism, however, the politics would not have found its proper theoretical expression (Althusser, 1974, pp 158, 160).

Here I am not concerned with Marx himself but with someone who claimed to have completed Marx's theory of the state. Even if one rejects this particular claim, Poulantzas certainly made major contributions to Marxist political analysis. Moreover his work reveals shifts in *theoretical* object which are remarkably similar to those of Marx himself. Both men moved from law to the state and thence to political economy. The shifts in Poulantzas's *political* position might seem less radical but they are nonetheless important. From an *existentialo marxiste* approach he tried to combine Althusserian philosophical positions and Gramscian political positions within an essentially Marxist-Leninist outlook and then went on to adopt a left Eurocommunist position similar

to that of pre-war Austro-Marxism. Naturally Marx and
Poulantzas also undertook rather different shifts in their
respective *philosophical* positions. Poulantzas moved from a
Sartrean approach through Althusserian structuralism to a
revolutionary materialism different in several respects from
that of Marx. Nonetheless his theoretical and political shifts
were more or less closely associated with shifts in philosophical position.

The interesting question here is, of course, whether these
philosophical shifts were as important for Poulantzas as for
Marx. What were the influences that permitted Poulantzas to
change his theoretical object and to develop his radically new
and important contributions to Marxist state theory? To
what extent did shifts in philosophical position express and/
or realise his theoretical innovations? What role did politics
play within this movement? These are the key issues on our
agenda.

The three sources of Poulantzas

Poulantzas's contributions to state theory depended on his
location at the confluence of three contrasting theoretical
streams. His originality lies in his unique synthesis of three
intellectual sources somewhat different from those that inspired Marx himself. In the case of Poulantzas these theoretical traditions were French – not German – philosophy;
Italian – not German – politics; and, not English economics,
not any economics, but Romano-German law. More specifically he drew successively on three French philosophical
traditions: first, Sartre and existentialism, then Althusser and
structuralism, and, finally, Foucault and the micro-physics
of power and strategy. In the field of Italian politics he was
influenced above all by Gramsci and, later, the Ingrao left (a
left Eurocommunist tendency in the Italian Communist Party). And, thirdly, in relation to Romano-German law, the
key influences were the Vienna school associated with Hans
Kelsen and, more generally, the constitutional and administrative law which he had acquired at Law Schools in Athens,
Munich, Heidelberg, and Paris.

Poulantzas went on to synthesise these sources in a unique
manner within the overarching framework of Marxist political economy. Poulantzas was, of course, influenced by

other theoretical sources. But they were filtered through the
three principal traditions. Thus Maoist themes were taken up
through an Althusserian perspective. Crucial Austro-
Marxist themes were likewise appropriated through their
influence in Italian political debate.

These different schools or traditions are combined and
developed in a quite specific manner within the context of
Marxist political economy. For Poulantzas firmly opposed
the traditions of the Second International and the Comin-
tern. Both allegedly reduced the nature of the state to a
simple reflection of the economic base and/or suggested that
political class struggles followed the course of economic
development. More generally Poulantzas notes that orthodox Marxism had systematically neglected the question of
the state. He attempts to remedy this. In particular Poulantzas emphasised the *sui generis* nature of political class struggle and the relative autonomy of the state. This is especially
clear in capitalist societies with their characteristic institutional separation between market and state, bourgeois and
citizen, private and public. Initially Poulantzas justified this
emphasis through a Sartrean approach to structural analysis.
Thus he employs the 'internal-external' dialectic to explore
the complex internal organisation of different social structures and their differential determination by external factors.
Later Poulantzas justified his concern with the political in
terms of Althusser's account of the relative autonomy of the
state within a complex 'structure in dominance' (sic) determined in the last instance by the economic. Eventually he
developed his own distinctive approach to the state as a social
relation, i.e., to state power as a form-determined condensa-
tion of the balance of forces in political class struggle.

As his work developed Poulantzas linked these arguments
more closely and coherently with traditional Marxist themes
in economic analysis. The latter had largely been ignored in
his early work. Indeed, as he himself readily admitted, he was
no expert in economics. Economic themes only came to
prominence in his work on *Classes in Contemporary Capitalism*. With his last major work on state theory, however,
Poulantzas had synthesised the three sources of his approach
firmly within the framework of classical Marxist political
economy.

But he also brought new insights to this framework. In

particular he considered the labour process in terms of a
complex economic, political, and intellectual division of
labour and examined social classes from the viewpoint of
their *extended* reproduction (sic) rather than in restricted
economic terms. At the same time he remained trapped
within classical Marxist political economy. At a time when
there was a general hue and cry about the 'crisis of Marxism',
Poulantzas remained committed to the determining role of
the mode of production and to the primacy of proleterian
class struggle in the transition to socialism. Only in his last
year did he begin seriously to question these fundamental
tenets of Marxism and try to move beyond them.

The philosophical preconditions of Poulantzas's theory

Althusser argued that Marx made his scientific breakthrough
by adopting specific class positions in philosophy as well as
politics. The three theoretical sources could only produce
the break because Marx took up proletarian political positions and proletarian philosophical positions. Does the same
hold true for Poulantzas?

This question is difficult to answer in these terms. In part
this is because Poulantzas was already working within the
Marxist tradition. But more basically I cannot accept that
philosophical positions are always aligned unambiguously
with class interest. Still less am I convinced that revolutionary materialism (whatever this might mean for Althusser) is
the only true *proletarian* philosophical position (whatever
this might mean). Furthermore Poulantzas himself came to
reject such essentialist readings of philosophy. He argued
that there was an inevitable gap between theory and practice
– Marxism did not lead to the Gulag any more than Catholicism led to the Spanish Inquisition or Francoism. Thus we
must consider all the mediations involved in any link between Poulantzas's changing philosophical positions and his
theoretical and political positions.

In his Sartrean phase Poulantzas's chief philosophical concern was to establish the unity of fact and value. But he also
drew on Sartre's method of dialectical reasoning to establish
the complex 'internal-external' determinations of bourgeois

law in terms of its own, *sui generis* properties and its overall position in capitalist societies. In turning to an Althusserian approach Poulantzas was mainly seeking to justify a separate political theory against more conventional base-superstructure arguments. Thus he drew heavily on Althusser's arguments about the movement from abstract to concrete, the overdetermination of concrete conjunctures, and the notion of relative autonomy. But there was little mileage to be derived from Althusser's philosophical position in developing the substantive concepts for a theory of the state. Here Poulantzas needed to supplement Althusserian concepts with others drawn from Italian Marxism and legal theory.

In his final theoretical phase Poulantzas adopted a *relational* approach. When he claimed to have discovered at last the Marxist theory of the state, he alluded to the idea that the state is a social relation. This involved a fundamental philosophical shift and a return to the revolutionary materialism of Marx. For it was Marx who elaborated the paradigmatic thesis (and arguably more general claim) that capital is a social relation. In progressively abandoning structuralism Poulantzas was influenced by Foucault. But this last shift is essentially rooted in the dynamic of his own thought and political involvements and its germs can already be seen in his first work on state theory.

Thus we can see that Poulantzas's changing theoretical and political positions were coupled with changes in philosophical positions. The latter were also fundamental *preconditions* of his theoretical innovations. For, although Poulantzas was mainly concerned with *political* rather than philosophical questions, changes in his ontological and/or methodological assumptions were crucial in mediating changes in his approach to the state and political strategy. In the specific conjuncture in which Poulantzas was working on *Political Power and Social Classes*, for example, his theoretical innovations could not have occurred without the influence of Althusserian structuralism. Some elements of his new approach occur in his earlier work on law, others in earlier remarks on hegemony. But they could only be adequately synthesised when their different institutional and strategic aspects were located at different levels in the movement from abstract to concrete as well as in relation to the overall structure of the capitalist system. In the intellectual and political conjuncture of France in the mid-sixties this framework could only be provided by Althusser. In this sense, just as Marx needed Feuerbach to move beyond Hegel, Poulantzas needed Althusser to move beyond Sartre. But Althusserian structuralism in its initial form also obstructed further theoretical and political advance. Thus Poulantzas needed to go beyond Althusser and to rediscover Marx's revolutionary materialism (or at least its 'relational' kernel) to develop his mature theory of the state.

I think that this stress on revolutionary materialism is correct. For, if Poulantzas's subsequent shift towards a relational theory of the state and a left Eurocommunist politics was associated with a move towards Foucauldian positions, the latter are nonetheless best interpreted as means through which new ideas were *expressed* rather than their essential precondition. Poulantzas certainly acknowledged the influence of Foucauldian language and ideas as he thought through new problems. But he also stressed that it was Foucault as an analyst of power – not Foucault as an epistemologist or methodologist – who inspired him. His philosophical breakthrough was his own. It involved both a fundamental return to Marx and a partial movement beyond him.

The motor-force of political involvements

We must also ask what drove Poulantzas beyond a philosophy of law written from the perspective of '*existentialo-marxisme*' to a hybrid Althusserian and Gramscian account of the state and thence to a left-wing Eurocommunist position. The key to this movement appears to be his involvement in Greek and French politics. Without this, as Althusser might have said, nothing would have happened. But it is equally clear that not all those involved in Greek or French politics developed Poulantzas's theoretical framework. His innovations presuppose both his involvement in three distinctive theoretical traditions and his commitment to a particular, Marxist method of theoretical and political analysis. They also presuppose changes in his philosophical position.

But what prompted these changes? I want to argue here

that it was his political involvements that provided the real motor force and that these depended on the course of political events beyond Poulantzas's control. Marx had to await the Paris Commune before he was finally able to work out his views on the 'dictatorship of the proletariat'. Likewise Poulantzas had to await the collapse of the Greek junta in 1974 before he could finally develop his views on the 'dictatorship of the bourgeoisie' and its implications for socialist strategy. Moreover, if it was by adopting proletarian political positions that Marx could make his major scientific breakthrough, a crucial factor for Poulantzas was his partial *abandonment* of a 'pure' proletarian class position. The latter characterised his Marxist-Leninist phase and prevented him from understanding the nature of politics in modern societies. Here Poulantzas had to await the collapse of the *Union de la Gauche* at the instigation of the PCF in 1977 before he could re-evaluate the leading role of the vanguard communist party and the working class in the struggle for socialism. Only then did he seriously consider popular-democratic struggles and the activities of the new social movements with their cross-class character. And not until then did he develop the full force of his strategy for a democratic transition to democratic socialism.

Thus Poulantzas's originality also depended on his attempts to understand and influence political events in Greece and France. For Greece his principal concern was to understand its military dictatorship, the conditions leading to its overthrow, the absence of working class hegemony in the democratisation process, and the prospects for moving from an anti-dictatorial alliance to an anti-imperialist, anti-monopoly alliance. Two key turning points for him were the Greek coup in April 1967 and its eventual collapse under the weight of its own internal contradictions in May 1974. The coup itself posed starkly the fundamental difference between democracy and dictatorship and also led to a more active political role for Poulantzas. The way in which the dictatorship collapsed, especially the absence of mass struggles directly concerned to confront the state, posed equally stark problems. It confirmed Poulantzas in his rapidly growing suspicion that the state was far from monolithic and that class struggle penetrated deep within the state itself. In turn this implied that a left Eurocommunist strategy aimed at inten-

sifying the contradictions internal to the state as well as
mobilising the popular masses outside the state could pre-
pare the ground for the eventual democratic transformation
of the state system as a whole.

This view was reinforced by the failure of the so-called
Portuguese Revolution despite the more favourable position
of left-wing forces in the initial struggle for power. For
Poulantzas was particularly scathing about the reformists'
attempts in Portugal simply to infiltrate the leading person-
nel of the state at the expense of mass struggle and the
ultra-left's equally misguided belief that socialism had arrived and that the state would simply wither away and could
therfore safely be ignored. Instead Poulantzas called for a
strategy which would democratise the state and permit it to
be used in defense of autonomous rank-and-file movements
at a distance from the state.

In relation to France, Poulantzas's concerns ranged from
the rise of authoritarian statism to the problems of left unity
around an anti-monopoly, democratic socialist programme.
May 1968 was a crucial moment for Poulantzas as for other
intellectuals in Paris. In subsequent years he became active in
the ideological struggle for left unity. Much of his work can
be seen as an attempt to provide the theoretical justification
for class alliances (especially between proletariat and new
petty bourgeoisie rather than between worker and peasant);
and, later, the theoretical justification for combining class
struggles with those of social movements. If the Greek coup
and its eventual collapse proved significant in some respects,
the struggle for left unity in France and its temporary collapse in 1977 proved significant in others. It was this latter
event that led Poulantzas to turn away from a simple faith in
proletarian struggles and the vanguard communist party and
towards a more complex and more problematic alliance
strategy which was not only *pluriclassiste* but also *pluripar-
tiste*, which denied any *a priori* privilege to the working class
or communist party, and which emphasised the autonomous
role of non-class forces and social movements in the struggle
for democratic socialism.

In this way Poulantzas arrived at his final 'Austro-
Marxist' political position. He called for a combination of
struggles at a distance from the state, within the state, and to
transform the state; and he advocated a combination of

representative and direct democracy as the best means to avoid the statist degeneration of socialism which had occured in the Soviet bloc. This final position was achieved because Poulantzas adopted positions in the political class struggle in both Greece and France. The surprises which events in these countries presented for him caused a continual re-appraisal of his political and theoretical positions and their interrelations. His continued efforts to understand these surprises led him to effect a new synthesis among his three theoretical traditions as well as to advocate a new political strategy.

Poulantzas moved from a Marxist-Leninist political strategy to a commitment to a left Eurocommunist strategy in which representative and direct democracy were to be combined and a key role was to be played by new social movements as well as traditional class forces and parties. He argued that only such a strategy could avoid the dangers of social democratic statism and soviet bureaucratic statism. Who could doubt the continued relevance of this strategy when one looks at events in the modern world? In this respect Poulantzas's legacy is still valid and still vital. But it would be wrong to ascribe this legacy solely to Poulantzas. He merely participated, after all, in a more general movement towards left Eurocommunist and Austro-Marxist political positions. More distinctive is his theoretical legacy. This concerns the approach to the state as a social relation and its implications for the analysis of state form, political class struggle, and their complex inter-relations. This legacy remained unclaimed for some time and it is only now that a subsequent generation of Marxist political theorists has begun to explore its implications. Let us hope that this work will continue.

Notes

L. Althusser, *Essays in Self-Criticism*, London, New Left Books, 1974.
P. Anderson, *Considerations on Western Marxism*, London, New Left Books, 1976.
B. Jessop, *Nicos Poulantzas: Marxist Theory and Political Strategy*, London, Macmillan, 1985.

N. Poulantzas, *Political Power and Social Classes*, London, New Left Books, 1973.

N. Poulantzas, *Fascism and Dictatorship*, London: New Left Books, 1974

N. Poulantzas, *Classes in Contemporary Capitalism*, London: New Left Books, 1975.

N. Poulantzas *Crisis of the Dictatorships, 2nd edn.*, London: New Left Books, 1976.

N. Poulantzas, *State, Power, Socialism*, London: New Left Books, 1978.

HISTORY IN FRANCE
Emmanuel Le Roy Ladurie

Today I am going to talk as a professional historian about the French school of history and make an assessment of its present and past achievements; at the end, I will discuss this type of history as juxtaposed with modern science. I am relatively competent as to the first task; relatively incompetent for the second. My attempt at comparison will inevitably make a call upon the 'lenience of the jury', but the inverse objection could be made to the exact scientist who deals with the relations between his own work and history, which he knows little of. So I am not in such bad company or in such a pitiful position as one might imagine.

A few words to start with concerning the evolution of French historiography. It may be said that, starting off with the 'event', our school of history then gave itself over to 'structures' or to 'long conjectures', returning, in the end, on occasion, to the event, but now seen in a different light. For a long time history was concerned with battles, with princely bedchambers, with catastrophes, whether minor or not. Then, in the inter-war period, it shifted to the study of structures and mentalities. The creation of the journal *Annales* in 1929 was only a starting-point; even so it gave an impetus to what we nowadays call, using a term which oversimplifies, 'the new history'. The *Annales* enterprise was launched in 1929 by Lucien Febvre and Marc Bloch. They were then Professors at the University of Strasbourg. The idea of studying civilization and customs instead of pure events is ancient: one can find it in Voltaire or Michelet, and also to be sure amongst non-French historians. When it comes to my country, a conception of this sort took on some importance beginning with Henri Berr and the *Revue de Synthese*, before the First World War.

As a student and *normalien*, Marc Bloch was influenced by Marxism, although he hardly ever acknowledged this debt in later life. For his part, Lucien Febvre took an interest in the French School of Human Geography. He combined a

historical approach with perspectives on the *present* organisation of the land: that allowed him, like our School of
Geography, to recognise the influence of the past in present-
day structures (think, for example, of the arrangement of
fields, of the open field, etc). It was in this spirit that in 1912
Lucien Febvre wrote his vast doctoral thesis, a thesis of a
very French type, on the Franche-Comté in the sixteenth
century. The 'big thesis' corresponds to a literary genre
which we, in France, sometimes speak of as a 'brick' or
'paving-stone'. After the First World War, Febvre and Bloch
met at Strasbourg, where the university was to receive every
possible assistance, following the restoration of Alsace to
France after the defeat of Germany. My compatriots intended to make large 'intellectual investments' in this province.

The *Annales* collection of the period after 1929 is not very
much read today, and that is a pity. A brief look at their
books may give us a sense of what the Founding Fathers of
the new historiography wished for. First, Marc Bloch: he
produced a work on the peasantry, *Les caractères originaux
de l'histoire rurale francaise* (1931) (*French Rural History: an
Essay on its Basic Characteristics,* 1966) an excellent example
of a study of the 'long duration' (*longue durée*) as regards the
organisation of work and society in the villages. Bloch also
produced a large work on feudal society. There he sought to
distinguish the ideal type of seigneurial systems from feudal
systems; the *seigniory* in effect deals with the relations of the
lord to the peasants; *feudalism,* a word which the Marxists
have abused, relates to the bonds which are established between the higher lords and their colleagues of a less elevated
rank; in short, the suzerains and the vassals. This distinction
between lord and fief, as a step forward, was invigorating.
Indeed, feudalism, was on occasion to become the new grail
of medievalists. What is more, in his *Rois thaumaturges (The
Royal Touch),* Bloch underlined the sacred and mysterious
aspects of royalty. In succeeding decades considerable
efforts both in anthropological and historical thinking were
made in this connection. There was the celebrated work of
Kantorowicz, *The King's Two Bodies,* which sparked further
thinking on the body as a symbol of the State. This medita-
tion is firmly in the line of the Bloch of the Royal Touch. It
was to be fruitful for a long time. But sometimes it became

counter-productive, to the extent that it was made use of in any old way. It seems to me that the State, above all the monarchical State, is too important an entity to be summed up in the concept of even the physical person of the monarch – or even in the entity of a double body. The body of the king is dressed too quickly.

Lucien Febvre's development was a little different: after his book on the Franche-Comté, which was in part devoted to the problems of a 'material' past, Febvre moved towards the history of mentalities, embodied in *The Problem of Unbelief in the Sixteenth Century: the Religion of Rabelais.* Let me briefly summarise the argument of this work. Certain historians of literature, like Abel Lefranc, wanted to show that Rabelais was an atheist or at least that he displayed a more or less camouflaged irreligion. On this point, Febvre put forward some striking rebuttals: in order to be an atheist, to start with one must, he declared, inhabit an intellectual environment which is capable of leading one's contemporaries to an ideology without God. That implies a certain measure and a certain quality of scientific knowledge. Now, this was not at all the case for Rabelais. The author of *Gargantua* still found himself, like his contemporaries, in the twilight of an intellectual Middle Ages. Did Febvre go too far in this direction? His book, published in 1942, has in the end some reactionary overtones. In fact certain indications go to show that there were some atheists, or at least pantheists, including some amongst peasants, in the sixteenth century and even – which is astonishing – in the Middle Ages. But when all is said and done, this is unimportant because the essential thing remains. With this work, Lucien Febvre was able to set out the concept and the practice of the history of mentalities.

Braudel and Labrousse

After the death of Marc Bloch, shot by the Germans, and in the period after the war, the editorship of *Annales* was taken over by Fernand Braudel, who cannot be separated from his peer Ernest Labrousse.

Braudel is celebrated in the world of historians and even well beyond on account of his admirable book, *The Mediterranean and the Mediterranean World in the Age of*

Philip II. This work swarms with economic and above all geographical history. Braudel transcends the limitations which are artificially imposed by event and battle history. He paints a global vision of Mediterranean civilisation in the sixteenth century with his three-stage construction: firstly, the *long term* (permanent geographical structures, transhumance, 'eternal' problems of subsistence, etc.); secondly, *secular trends* such as those concerning the importing of American silver, the price revolution in Spain, etc.; finally, the short-term *event*: battles, diplomatic manoeuvres. With this three-fold base, Braudel's book is recognised by our profession to be of primary importance. The concept of the long term has been extremely useful. However, in a way it represents an empty form: in consequence one has to supply it *a posteriori* with some empirical content. Disrespectfully, I have sometimes spoken of the long term as an empty petrol tank. The same thing can be said of the notion of *episteme* in Foucault, or the *unsurpassable horizon* of Sartre, and of the *paradigm* of Thomas Kuhn. These vast givens correspond to long periods in the course of which a unique concept or a structured group of concepts globally dominates the entire fabric of science and/or mentalities. Nonetheless, one is obliged to explain such a concept or group, and give it a precise definition in every case. If this operation is not put into effect, the episteme, the paradigm and even the long term duration remain simply empty vessels.

Braudel also drew an immense personal energy from his species of spontaneous materialism, which, to my way of thinking, he pushed a bit too far in the end. He expressed scarcely any interest in the social history of religions and for the main part applied himself to the study of material culture in the broad sense of this term. From this point of view, and even though he never gave any sign of having a grand passion for the thought of Karl Marx, the French thinker was not entirely at the opposite end of the spectrum from a certain sort of Marxism. Able Marxists like I. Wallerstein have gained much from this strong relative proximity and made use, indeed manipulated, the work or the person of Braudel. Take a look in this connection at a text of Wallerstein's in the journal entitled *Radical History Review* (Vol XXVI, 1982). He succeeds here in writing about Braudel as if Lenin, Stalin and Trotsky really counted as theoreticians for the historian of the Mediterranean! Braudel is the source of an extraordinary paradox: he magisterially analyses and depicts the Mediterranean of the 16th century, without taking into account the differences which exist between Islam and Catholicism[1] in terms of economic performance.

Ernest Labrousse, another historian of importance although less known internationally, turned out to be of enormous influence after the War, with respect to the Annales school, of which, however, he was not a member in the strictest sense. He has the immense merit of making 'numbers' credible in French historiography, and especially at the Sorbonne. Up till then, the latter remained sceptical vis-a-vis the 'quantitative'.

The work of Labrousse consists essentially in two vast and grand books; together, they represent his double doctoral thesis (the giant thesis is one of the strangest institutions of the French University, and it is not as much a thing of the past as many people from abroad appear to think). The first of Labrousse's theses, for the Faculté de Droit, deals with the history of prices in the 18th century. There the author demonstrates that this period, above all after 1735, was contemporaneous with a long period of rising prices. It corresponded to a prosperous phase, of increases in rents and profits. It is true that this growth of market prices, and especially those of grain, could also be explained by the fact that the supply of wheat was not always sufficient, when one compares it with the concomitant rise in general demand for basics. These growing demands stemmed in fact from demographic expansion: the latter forced the farmers into making their grain dearer, and making it more and more difficult for consumers to get hold of, since the actual number of the latter was increasing. From whence a movement of inflation of prices. As for wages, they went into a decline in relation to the cost of living. On account of this, one finds the proliferating proletariat suffering from pauperisation.

Labrousse's other thesis (a major work, like the preceding one) was produced for the Faculté des Lettres in Paris. It dealt with the economic crisis before the French Revolution, roughly under Louis XVI. This enormous inquiry attempts to show that, in that period, for some fifteen years, there was a severe fall in prices. This interrupted or at least hindered economic growth which had proceeded without too much difficulty, from 1715 until 1774. Hence the depression from 1775 on represents one of the numerous 'causes' which provoked popular discontent and in its turn, helped to trigger off the Revolution of 1789. Elected to the Sorbonne, Labrousse had a large number of students. The centralised system of our nation made it possible for this excellent historian to attract first class students. They were to situate themselves in the same current of thought and extend his researches in quantitative history.

In this connection a little bit of intellectual genealogy is useful. Pierre Goubert was one of the first students of Labrousse. The studies of prices had impressed him. At the same time, just like Louis Henry, Goubert embarked on the deciphering of parish registers, so as to reconstitute, with their aid, a historical demography. His book on the Beauvaisis, a small region of Northern France, was the model of the local monograph, with a historical base that is totally material, serial, social. This research was almost entirely devoid of the 'event' (if one puts to one side the famine of 1693). In the course of a work such as this, Goubert studied prices, social structures and, to a certain extent, the economy as discrete elements or symptoms of a unified system. From then on, a global view became possible with respect to the system within which the reproduction (in the broad sense) of the lower classes came about under the Ancien Regime. What was at stake in the facts was a model of simple reproduction. Two parents, father and mother, in this Beauvaisis of the time of Louis XIV, produced numerous children. Most of them died. In the end, only two of the young stayed the course, surviving to the age of twenty-five. In their turn, they married. They thus brought about reproduction without any addition to the initial situation. Two young people, in sum, succeeded two old ones. As a result, the population did not increase. It became legitimate, at the time, to talk of 'simple reproduction'.

Urban history

A pupil of Labrousse (also inspired by the researches of Goubert), Pierre Deyon, decided to transplant to an urban environment what had until then essentially been the rural mode of studies that the historian of the Beauvaisis practised.

He chose Amiens, an industrial city, made up of textile manufacturers or artisans during the 17th century. This is one of the first French essays in urban history. The scientific descriptions of a city's past had for a long time, up until Deyon, been considered as an English or American speciality, and not at all 'our sort of thing'.

The work of Deyon also dealt with the industrialisation of the countryside. We know that the peasants near the towns of Holland and Picardy busied themselves on behalf of urban merchants in order to produce thread and cloth. These goods, were in turn exported by the city-dwelling dealers to markets both near and far – as far as Latin America. The inquiry into Amiens converges with similar attempts conducted a little later by Frank Mendels in Flanders and by Hans Medick in Germany. We could speak in this connection of a theme of *protoindustrialisation*, which emerges as an original stage in the construction of capitalism. The industrialisation of the country, in fact, preceded the industrial revolution of the towns and the suburbs. The latter was to dominate our 19th and 20th centuries, since nothing better turned up.

Urban history started in France later than in the United States. In that large country, historians like Thernstrom had already produced important books. After Deyon, France had other studies of the same sort. I am thinking, for example, of Maurice Garden's thesis on Lyon in the 18th century, a town in which the silk industry was the primary activity. Here Garden found a quite specific urban demography during the Enlightenment. At that time, the middle and lower middle class Lyonnais sent their babies out to wet-nurses. This practice seemed economically feasible. As a consequence, young mothers with families did not benefit from the temporary sterility which statistically characterises women when they are feeding their children with their own milk. Hence these Rhone country mums had one pregnancy *a year* instead of one *every two years*. 'Biennial rotation' was in fact an advantage, for the young women who fed their children themselves. With annual childbirth a high percentage of the overnumerous little beings produced on the banks of the Rhone at such a pace died in the home of their wet-nurses. In reading Garden, these structures emerge as an example of urban pathology in what is already an industrial situation.

Everything took place in Lyons as if the demographic motor turned frighteningly fast and at the same time consumed too much. Nevertheless the final result is not that different from what happened in a non-pathological system, when it comes to the number of children who survived in the final account. In Lyon one has high fertility and high infant mortality. In the country one has lower fertility and lower mortality. The number of survivors per family is *grosso modo* analogous in the two cases. But the human cost of the system is larger in the town.

Another instance of urban history is the large work of Jean-Claude Perrot on Caen, an 18th century town in Lower Normandy. Local circumstances here turned out to be different from those exposed by Garden. In one sense, Perrot's book has scarcely any conceptual unity. He raises all manner of problems connected with what remained a relatively moderate rate of urban growth. Yet his two heavy volumes, the fruit of almost twenty years of research and editing, give us an excellent, perfectly calculated, description of the way in which a pre-Balzacian, petit-bourgeois city, without much industry, arrived at a certain equilibrium in 18th century Normandy, where the engine of progress never raced too fast. A sort of creative archaism prevailed.

Now for a couple of words about quantitative history, introduced into France by Jean Meuvret amongst others, in connection with the behaviour of prices in the seventeenth century. These researches are characterised by an extraordinary concern with minutiae. The theme that is today so well known, in France and elsewhere, of the crisis of the 17th century was popularised by Meuvret. Econometric methods, notably in the United States, have nowadays rendered out-of-date the techniques of Jean Meuvret, which, while being refined, were primitive, or at least artisanal. It is sad that this econometric sophistication, so intensely engaged in on the other side of the Atlantic, has not always been fertile. Take a look at the recent controversy about the work of Robert Fogel dealing with slavery. The 'cliometric' minutiae are pertinent, to be sure, to the study of the 19th century, about which we already possess good statistical bases. In contrast, econometry should not excuse the historians from establishing serious quantitative series for specific givens, such as those of prices, grain production, real salaries, etc., apropos of periods in the more distant past. In these more distant times, the quantitative publications of the State, for statistical and administrative usages, are scarcely to be found, as future 'sources' for historians.

Another approach: one can find in this French historiography of structures and conjunctures, so far from traditional research about events, a certain number of distinctive traits. I am thinking in particular about the use of cartography, which is nowadays subject to information processing. Thanks to work which is rounded off by the computer, one may project quantitative data on religious enthusiasm, height, literacy, etc., onto a ground map. French historians have a good geographical education. They have made great use of these techniques of spatial visualisation of statistical facts.

The New History and Marxism

It is not out of place to point out the links between French historiography of the new sort and Marxism. This grand theory raises extremely complex questions as well as complex matters of individual conscience. On the one hand, Marx's doctrine has degenerated – was this perhaps inevitable? It has become degraded to the point where it is used as a support for those modes of behaviour of totalitarian States that are most open to criticism. I will not say much about this problem, which is well known. But, on the other hand, in its distinctive forms Marxist thought contains many interesting elements. Sometimes it has been fruitfully employed in building up a scientific history. The work of Pierre Vilar is an example of this. Vilar studied the economic history of Catalonia. This north-eastern province of Spain was able to develop its commerce and industry well before the rest of the Iberian peninsula. (The other example of early, powerful development in the 'Spains' is to be found in the Basque country, which is also situated in the northerly part of the country.) In reflecting about Catalonia in the 18th century, Vilar was one of the first in France to make use of the concept of economic growth in quantitative terms for a period some distance in the past. He showed that Catalonia, and even Spain, did not go into decline in the 18th century, as purely political history tended to make one think. On the contrary, the peninsula experienced vigorous growth which was in its turn paralleled, or was more rapid than, the movement of rising prices. *Real* wages increased! 'Every ship floated up on the tide', those of capitalists and proletarians alike. In passing, note that Vilar is a Marxist and, although entirely humanistic, is even a *de facto* determined, self-proclaimed Stalinist. He has at no time hesitated in his most recent publications in lauding Stalin, as if the dictator had not been the person we know him to have been. Perhaps here we have an example of a split personality when it comes to the science of the past. Vilar, the admirable historian of the Ancient Regime, never hesitates in dogmatising when it comes to the 20th century. It is an extremely good thing that he remains empirical, with a dash of pertinent theory, when it comes to the 18th century.

Nonetheless, Vilar has immense merits. Many Marxists or Communist historians since the 1950s have followed an ideological or voluntaristic line. Vilar was one of those who encouraged young researchers to go more deeply into what is best at the core of the Marxist tradition – I mean attention paid to economic facts, to the behaviour of the masses, etc. For this and for several other reasons, the damage inflicted by Marxist-Leninism and by other 'made-to-measure' ideologies remained relatively superficial within the field of French historiography. Outside the properly historical sector, amongst the social sciences of my country and especially in university teaching, parrot-like Marxism was often to have negative effects.

Science and history

In the main, French historiography has remained faithful to a factual, I would even go so far as to say positivist, tradition – if this word hadn't for a long time been held to be contrary to the spirit of the *Annales* school and synonymous with the history of events. In reality, such an identification of *positivism* and the *event* is highly debatable. The very strong sense of the factual does not in any way mean that our historians are lacking in ideas, but simply that they haven't found it difficult to reject these initial models at a later time, if they proved themselves incapable of being adapted to reality. They were then obliged to propose other models, ones which proved to be more relevant for dealing with the problem at hand.

Is that to say that historians have gone as far as scientists along the road of a history which would be constructed on the basis of initial hypotheses, which must then be either confirmed or falsified by research? The econometric historians or the American cliometrists are happy to say that one must approach a specific historical problem, whatever it may be, a document or a sector, with a preconceived hypothesis. Then it is advisable to test the latter and then to concede, on the basis of the research thus put to the test, that the hypothesis in question is adequate; or, on the contrary, that it must be rejected as a result of the facts. These cliometricians, thus on occasion servilely imitate the procedures employed by the exact sciences. I am thinking, in connection with the latter, of astronomy, where, theoretically, one can define, given the physical parameters, a certain type of star that no-one has ever seen before. Then one reaches for the telescope and, finally, after extensive research, one perceives somewhere in the sky a stellar body of this sort. This is, of course, something of a caricature. In contrast, when it comes to its procedures of validation, history in part still belongs to the domain of the humanities. It never – or not in the true sense – proceeds in the rigorous style of the hard sciences.

So what does really go on in our research? Historians find themselves interested in a period or a document. They entertain some preconceived, or even hasty, ideas about it, or even perhaps no ideas at all. When such ideas exist (and in a certain sense, they always exist, even if subconsciously), historians carry these with them at that very moment when they try to decipher the deep meaning of the text which interests them. Whether explicit or *a fortiori* implicit, the initial hypothesis may prove to be false, superficial, inadequate or simply insufficient. At the next stage, researchers modify, adjust, or decisively reject, the hypothesis in question. They then discover or conjecture at other models which would be better adapted to the historical context under investigation. They may dream up the new *model* just like that, or, as is more frequently the case, they may take it from an author or thinker who has already formulated it. For example, they may reject in part or *in toto* the Marxist model, and wish to adopt notions taken from Malthus. That is what happened to me at one time. Or they may all of a sudden grow interested in the seminal ideas of Louis Dumont on inequality. But very often things do not come about with any scientific rigour even if the general drift is towards that. Quite simply, pure erudition persists alongside conceptual or conceptualised history.

I must also say a word or two about the practices of other social sciences within contemporary historiography. The *Annales* school and related groups have behaved in a variety of ways with respect to the social sciences. We need here to make a distinction between the three generations of the *Annales*, that of Febvre and Bloch, that of Braudel, and that of historians like Le Goff, etc. The first and second generations were above all inspired by economics and demography, sometimes by a rather rustic and simplistic economics. (I am thinking of the example of Simiand's theories on the A and B phases: A phases are those during which prices and profits rise. In contrast, B phases, like the seventeenth century, are characterised by a fall in prices and benefits, hence they are epochs of 'general crisis', exactly like the 17th century.) Afterwards, Marx, Malthus, Rostow, Kusnets, with their descriptions of growth, supplied Clio with other models and sources of inspiration. The case of demography has been the most distinctive: 'historical demography', in fact, has created its own methods, if not its own theoretical models. Be that as it may, it is significant that the demographer who invented the latter, Louis Henry, was not a professional historian but a *polytechnicien*. As a consequence, even in this case, Clio's man or woman remains dependent on the contributions accruing from the more exact or harder sciences.

Since 1968 or 1970, the tone has somewhat changed. Economic history and demography, to be sure, have maintained their thrust. In this connection I would mention researchers like Franklin Mendels or John Day, the latter being the admirable chronicler of the monetary crisis of the 15th century. However, the need for what Pierre Chaunu calls a 'systematic history of the third level' is felt more and more. In simplistic terms, the first level corresponds to the economy; the second, to society; the third, as a result, deals with culture and mentalities. In this context, culture is intended in a broad anthropological sense.

Was this historiographical mutation linked to the events

of May 1968? They certainly created a certain distrust of technocracy and computers, even and perhaps above all when employed in history. An unjustified distrust, I feel. But it is as a result of this, and a fortunate result it is, that the history of mentalities from then on takes on a new dynamism with men like Flandrin and Vovelle, Flandrin being interested in the history of the family and Vovelle in a quantitative chronology of attitudes to death in the 18th century. The influence of anthropologists like Redfield and Victor Turner, proved extremely important for these new movements in French historiography.

From a certain point of view, the history that was engendered, either legitimately or putatively, by the *Annales* school has dominated the intellectual field for fifteen or so years in my country. As historians, we are obliged to be somewhat 'democratic'. Hence we admit that certain non-scientific forms of our craft may on occasion be important for a global appreciation of historiographical phenomenon, at least as regards the impact of history on the larger public. In this connection, we have experienced, as it were, several 'rings' of influence. The outermost ring is that of the diffusion of a vulgar or popularised history; it restricts itself to the event; it is carried out by 'vulgarisers' of various qualities whom we hear and see a great deal of on the radio and television. Their contribution does not always yield anything of very great intellectual interest. Sometimes it diminishes, metaphorically, the treasure-house of human knowledge. Nonetheless, paradoxically, it has made the public receptive to more sophisticated historical categories. Another 'ring', more internal and more serious, is to be found in the media's dissemination of a species of scientific history. I am thinking of the radio programme *Lundi de l'Histoire* and also, in another branch of the media, of the articles published in this field in *Le Monde* and the *Nouvel Observateur*. Finally, at the centre of this system of dissemination, there are the very lively and varied paperback series. Thanks to these, history of the *Annales* type has been communicated to thousands, eventually to tens or hundreds of thousands of readers, within the academic market and beyond.

In various ways, history has come closer to the sciences. In certain respects, it remains a fabric of events, linking together causal chains which are often unique and particular. However it strives to attain to the repeatable, to the general, to the universal. *It aims to become more scientific,* and in any case more rigorous. At the same time, from another point of view, it has become more popular, closer to the masses, to the media, to a sizeable public, without for all that denying itself.

Let us enlarge the scope of the debate. On its side, science is becoming more historical, it is no longer solely in search of general laws, it is henceforth inquiring into the event, into the unique or rare occurrence which, when articulated in this or that causal chain, makes up a history. In short, history and science are each bridging that half of the gap which separates them from each other, or at least they are both tending towards this mutual consummation. History seems more scientific than it was in the past and science more concerned with the event. In this new form, science, as well, takes on aspects which are more popular, more familiar to a large number of 'consumers' of science, who are not personally researchers. So there is a convergence between the two great fields of knowledge, and our epoch is hungry for science for reasons which are not so different from those which make it crave history.

Let me explain myself. Astrophysics is no longer simply the knowledge of the eternal wheeling of the planets around a Newtonian sun. It now involves a revelation about our origins: it teaches us about the unique and gigantic event of the 'big bang' which launched our universe twenty billion years ago. Scientists date the birth of the solar system a little closer to home: – 4.57 billion years. After that a sequence of unique events is said to have unfolded. One cannot at the moment test them on other planets or on other solar systems. These events – sometimes the products of chance, like the birth of life; sometimes borrowed from a subsequent logic, like the apparition of oxygen, the coming into existence of aerobic vegetation, of animals, and finally of man – these processes are interrupted from time to time by ruptures like the one (which was perhaps catastrophic) which marked the transition from the Cretaceous to the Tertiary Era. These facts accrue to our sciences thanks to new techniques for the determination of time. Researchers work, when it is a question of the last five billion years, with radioactive dating methods. Once discovered, these extremely precise chronological results elicit the curiosity of readers or spectators. Tens of thousands, sometimes even more, enthuse over the books of Reeves or of Weinberg, of Chaunu, Morin, Ruffie. Millions watch the 'scientific' programmes of Carl Sagan on the TV screens of several countries.

The double convergence, scientised history, historicised science, rests on certain convergences as to the conceptions that can be had of the diverse varieties of Time. To start off with there is the lived time of the individual, its non-historical, psychological duration, limited by birth and death. There is also – and this is what interests me here – the 'expert' time of the historians and the exact sciences, based in the former on the collective reconstitution of traces brought with or left by the artificially regrouped testimony of great numbers of past individuals, unknown or famous, and in the latter on the geological or astronomical flow of stellar or terrestial events recorded in nature. After all, a dating using Carbon 14 is an indifferent sign. It can signal the non-human construction of a moraine by a glacier in the thousand years before Christ, or of the remains of a hut abandoned by men in the Iron Age.

The double convergence that I mentioned thus leads to global sequences which have some relation with each other. The spectacle of *growth*: it starts with the triumphal expansion which follows the cosmic 'big bang' or it is embodied in the successive take-offs of economics and demography. On both sides prodigious results are recorded. But, on the cosmic side, everything will finally tend to be dissipated at the end of time in explosions which will mark the end of the solar system or in the indefinite and fatal expansion of the universe. On the other side, in a much briefer temporal span, on the side of the human species, we are troubled by the accumulation of pollution, of excess of population, of a possible return of barbarity or by nuclear annihilation. There is no definitive consolidation of progress.

In this sense the present day situation of our historico-scientific (or 'historicised-scientised') knowledge, edified for the initiated but just as much for the larger public, makes one think of other conjunctures. My reference here is to the maturity and then the decline of the Roman Empire when Judeo-Christian ideas were worked out and then triumphed. For the overly fixed conceptions of the science of Antiquity, centred on universal laws or even on the eternal return, Judeo-Christianity substituted infinitely more historical sequences, seasoned by an entire chronological schema with linear time: creation of the world, redemption, final catastrophe and last judgement. In their own way, the scientists and historians of today are like the Judeo-Christians, who were ignorant or who in certain cases knew themselves to be such. Across the discontinuities, the permanence of a certain culture is thus affirmed. The scientists and the historians of our time like that of the Judeo-Christians react against a world which was sure of itself for too long and henceforth the world felt itself to be inhabited by the anxiety of its own destruction. Once again, there was a challenge to an immobile science whose models, drawn from Newtonian mechanics, did not give sufficient space to the time of origins. So they proposed schemas whose explosive origin the faithful were a little too hasty in comparing to the Creation and the free-thinkers were indignant to see defined as if it were a question of the Book of Genesis. Following this, scientists and historians marked out the unique stages of a majestic expansion and of a redemptive progress. The latter for a long time seemed irresistible.

Today we regard so-called 'progress' with the rigour that it requires. We are now weighed down with a future of anxiety – one which is close to being dissipated in a few billion years in the termination of the universe. On the planet Earth, it could come to an end much quicker than that, in the uncontrollable unreason of a humanity beset by demographic explosion, by nuclear proliferation, by the dangers of the final extermination, or in a decline into barbarism and/or totalitarianism. When all is said and done, both historians and scientists have the presentiment of a last judgement. Yet they profess a certain scepticism with respect to the promises of an individualised eternal life. Will those of bad faith object that eternity is not in time? We will be wary of listening to them.

Notes

1.   There is no point in mentioning in this connection the Protes-

tantism one finds in Max Weber; there are no Protestants in the countries bordering on the Mediterranean, except in Languedoc.

2.   K. Papaioannou, *La consecration de l'histoire*, Paris: Editions Champ Libre, 1983, p.70 etc.

A DIFFERENCE IN MENTALITIES
Peter Burke

Any account of historical writing in France and Britain over
the last sixty years or so needs to avoid the temptation to
make too strong or too simple a contrast between France and
Britain. There are of course genuine and important differences between the historical paradigms dominant on the two
sides of the Channel, but these differences are of several
different kinds. There is the contrast between philosophical
traditions, for example. The styles of historical writing
dominant on the two sides of the Channel do have something
to do with the old contrast between British empiricism and
French rationalism, between British methodological individualism and French holism, John Stuart Mill or Herbert
Spencer versus Emile Durkheim, or even Locke versus De-
scartes. One can pinpoint the contrast by referring to the
British suspicion of the *histoire des mentalités,* a term it is
still impossible to translate smoothly into English. On one
side, the view that 'there is no such thing as the history of
mentalities, but only the history of individuals thinking; on
the other, the view that a mentality is not a thing at all, but a
relationship between beliefs and assumptions.

However, the contrast between Britain and France cannot
be reduced to this philosophical infrastructure (or, dare I say,
this difference in mentalities). There is also a contrast, which
has not been sufficiently stressed, between French centralisa-
tion and British pluralism. Lucien Febvre and Marc Bloch
were successful revolutionaries who captured the Establishment. Febvre was the first to rule the kingdom of *Annales,*
Braudel was the second, and Emmanuel Le Roy Ladurie is
third in succession. The centre of the system is in Paris. In
Britain, on the other hand, the historiographical regime is
much more decentralised. Oxford, Cambridge and London
go their own ways. If we look at the same three generations
on this side of the Channel, we find a situation which was
much more pluralistic, or simply messy.

In the age of Bloch and Febvre, traditional narrative political history was still the dominant mode in Britain, but alternatives did exist. One group of rebels were entrenched in their fortress in Houghton St, the London School of Economics. Their leader was R.H. Tawney and their banner was inscribed 'Economic History Review', but they were interested in social as well as economic history, and more generally in structure and process rather than in events. At Manchester there was Lewis Namier, a highly individual blend of radicalism and conservatism. An immigrant, an East-Central European intellectual but in some ways more English than the English, Namier was a political historian to the core but one who broke with the conventions of historical narrative. He could be described as an analytical, structural, prosopographical, social historian of politics.

In the second generation, the coexistence of different historical sub-cultures is still more obvious. After the Second World War, a group of historians centred on the journal *Past and Present* and largely inspired by an open Marxism, went further in new directions than either Tawney or Namier had done. They challenged the dominant paradigm, met it head-on, offered a complete alternative. Hill and Hilton, Hobsbawn and Thompson are too well known to need further comment. Meanwhile another group, which kept a lower profile and based themselves in a quiet provincial town, at the University of Leicester, were developing an alternative approach to social history. They saw social history as local history and local history as social history. Their leader, W.G. Hoskins, deserves recognition (a recognition he does not seem to have received outside Britain) as a sort of homespun Braudel, concerned like him with 'geohistory' in his *Making of the English Landscape,* and with *la longue duree* (at village scale) in his *Midland Peasant.* A third group (based in Cambridge, though not in the Faculty of History), were working on historical demography in a manner not far removed from that of the French: the Cambridge Group for the History of Population and Social Structure. A fourth sub-culture, in which a distinctive style of cultural history was being developed, was that of a group working at the Warburg Institute, formerly of Hamburg, now a foreign body lodged in the University of London. Although she was not well known, Frances Yates was doing some of her best work at the Institute in the 1940s and 1950s.

In the second generation, contacts with French historians remained infrequent, although Richard Cobb was trying to create a second identity as a Frenchman. Braudel's *Mediterranean* remained untranslated, and more Hungarian and Polish historians wrote for *Annales* than British ones did. Paris seemed closer to Budapest and Warsaw than to London. In the third generation, starting in the middle of the 1960s, the leading French hisorians began to appear in English (or at least in American). Whether they approve or not, most professional historians and a fair number of amateurs now have some idea of what the French are doing, from Georges Duby on the medieval family to Maurice Agulhon on nineteenth-century politics. Among the more recent British historical sub-cultures, of which the best known is History Workshop, there is also a group of fellow travellers of *Annales* in which I would include myself, a group which is conscious of a great intellectual debt owed to Bloch and Braudel and Emmanuel Le Roy Ladurie.

In this third generation, there has been some convergence of interests between French and British historians. The interest in urban history seems to have grown up independently on both sides of the Channel, like the interest in popular culture and historical anthropology. Contrasts remain. Keith Thomas's approach to witchcraft is not the same as that of Robert Mandrou or Robert Muchembled, just as Jim Dyos's style of urban history differed from that of Maurice Garden. Exactly what each side has to learn from the other is hard to say. I can think of British historians who still have everything to learn from *Annales,* but others have assimilated a great deal already. As for the French, until a few years ago it was possible to reproach them with their neglect of politics; the masthead of *Annales* was inscribed *économies, sociétés, civilisations* but made no mention of *états.* The masthead has not changed but Emmanuel Le Roy Ladurie and other have rediscovered Louis XIV.

Perhaps this is one sign among others that *Annales* is fading out as an independent movement: in the life of a movement, three generations is a long time. Its identity is threatened by its success; the group is becoming less and less distinctive. But there are also signs of some kind of backlash, not only a rediscovery of politics but also what Lawrence Stone has called the 'revival of narrative'. Whether this is a good or a bad thing depends of course on the kind of narrative, whether it is an incorporation of analysis or an abdication from it. Perhaps it is a new kind of narrative that we need now. The American critic Hayden White looks forward to the day when historians write like Kafka or Joyce, but more appopriate models might be Proust or Claude Simon.

In other words, learning from the French ought not to be restricted to learning from Bloch or Braudel. Some British historians have in fact found something of value for their work in Claude Levi-Strauss and Pierre Bourdieu. Still more have been tempted, and also teased, by the ideas of the late Michel Foucault, whom historians regard as a philosopher though philosophers treat him as a historian. To speak personally, I find it equally impossible to accept Foucault's methods and his conclusions, yet continue to believe that historians have much to learn from him, from the perverse originality with which he turned conventional assumptions on their heads. Once this has been done, the historical world never looks the same again. Even if the inverted assumptions are no more tenable than the original ones, we owe Foucault a great deal for making us so vividly aware of alternatives.

NOTES ON CONTRIBUTORS

Michèle Barrett is author of *Women's Oppression Today* and co-author of *The Anti-social Family*.

Ted Benton is the author of *The Rise and Fall of Structural Marxism*.

Malcolm Bradbury's many books include *Rates of Exchange* and *The History Man*.

Peter Burke is the author of *Popular Culture in Early Modern Europe* and *Sociology and History*.

Christian Descamps is lecturer at the University of Paris and author.

Peter Dews is the author of *Logics of Disintegration*.

Terry Eagleton's many books include *Myths of Power, Criticism and Ideology* and *The Function of Criticism*.

John Forrester is the author of *Language and the Origins of Psychoanalysis* and the forthcoming *The Dream of Psychoanalysis*.

Bob Jessop is the author of a forthcoming book on Nicos Poulantzas.

Cora Kaplan is currently working on *A Romantic Twist of the Mind: Feminism, Class and Literature in the 19th Century*.

Emmanuel Le Roy Ladurie is the author of *Montaillou, Love, Death and Money in the Pays D'Oc*, and *Territory of the Historian* amongst other books.

Jacques Roubaud, poet and mathematician, is a member of the Collège International de Philosophie.

Alan Sheridan is the translator of Foucault into English and the author of *The Will to Truth*.

Gareth Stedman Jones is the author of *Languages of Class* and the forthcoming *From Marx to Marxism*.

Jeffrey Week's books include *Coming Out* and *Sexuality and its Discontents*.

This new edition of *Ideas from France: The Legacy of French Theory* was commissioned by Robert M. Young and produced by Martin Klopstock for Free Association Books. It was finished in October 1989.

This edition was printed on a 15 Harris web on to 80g/m² vol.18 Publishers Antique Wove.